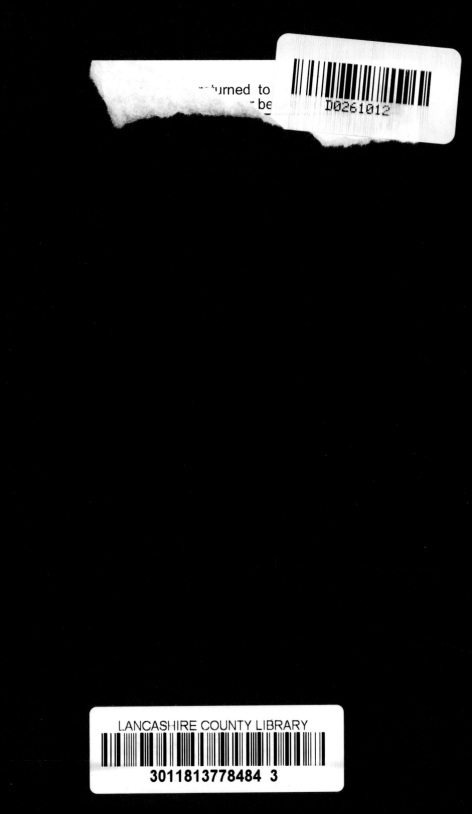

~~returned to~~
~~be~~

D0261012

Crimson

Crimson

NIVIAQ KORNELIUSSEN

Translated by Anna Halager

virago

VIRAGO

First published in Greenland in 2014 as *HOMO sapienne*
by Milik Publishing
First published in Great Britain in 2018 by Virago Press

1 3 5 7 9 10 8 6 4 2

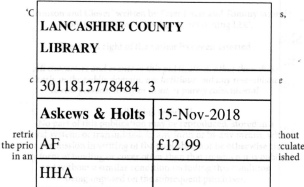

A CIP catalogue record for this book
is available from the British Library.

Hardback ISBN 978-0-349-01057-1
Export ISBN 978-0-349-01055-7

Typeset in Minion by M Rules
Printed and bound in Great Britain by
Clays Ltd, Elcograf S.p.A.

Papers used by Virago are from well-managed forests
and other responsible sources.

Virago Press
An imprint of
Little, Brown Book Group
Carmelite House
50 Victoria Embankment
London EC4Y 0DZ

An Hachette UK Company
www.hachette.co.uk

www.virago.co.uk

Qaaqa ('big sister')

All I can say is thank you
Simply for being my sister
Simply for enriching my world to the fullest
Simply for being you

Your world is mine
My world is yours

Nuka ('little sister')

Contents

Cast of Characters

Fia

Fia is Inuk's sister and Arnaq's short-term flat mate. She is in a relationship with Peter and studies at the university.

Inuk

Means 'human'/'man' as in 'mankind' in Greenlandic, but is also commonly used as a name for men (sometimes also for women).

Inuk works as a journalist in Nuuk until he moves to Denmark. He is Fia's brother and Arnaq's best friend.

Arnaq

Means 'woman' in Greenlandic, but is also commonly used as a name.

Arnaq is Inuk's best friend, and also works as a journalist until she gets fired. Fia, Inuk's sister, is staying with Arnaq.

Ivik

Ivik is a Greenlandic name that means 'a blade of grass', and is commonly used for men, but with the diminutive suffix '-nnguaq' it means 'dear little Ivik' and becomes a commonly used name for women.

Ivik is Sara's partner.

Sara

Sara is in a relationship with Ivik. Her older sister is pregnant, and Sara is waiting for her first nephew or niece to be born.

Crimson

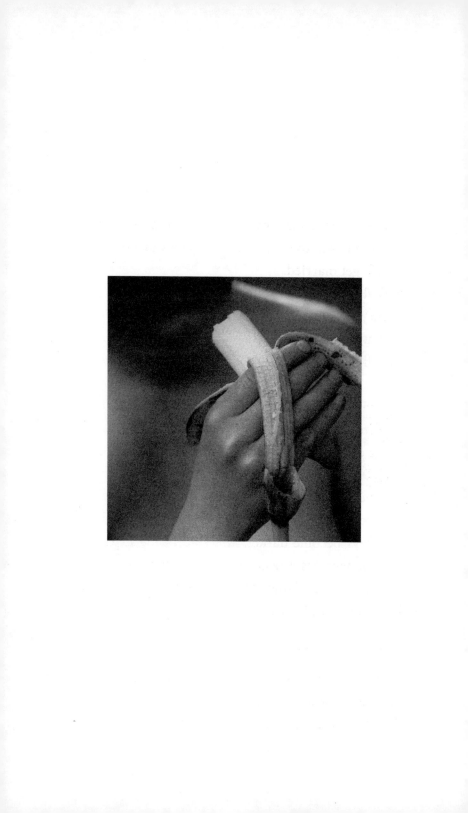

Our plans:

1. When I've finished my education and have the money, we'll buy a house with lots of rooms and a balcony.
2. We'll get married.
3. We'll have three or four kids.
4. Every day, we'll go shopping after work and drive home in our car.
5. We'll get old and die.

Peter. One man. Three years. Thousands of plans. Millions of dinner invitations. Vacuuming, dishwashing and cleaning, rushing on forever towards infinity. False smiles turning uglier. Dry kisses stiffening like desiccated fish. Bad sex should be avoided at all costs. My faked orgasms get harder to believe as time goes by. But we're still making plans.

The days become darker. The void in me expands. My love no longer has a taste. My youth's turning old. What keeps me alive is dying. My life has become worn, aged. Life? What life? My heart? It's a machine.

'What're we having for supper?'

Sticky pig's tails, which reminds me of what you have in your pants, is what I want to reply.

'What are you doing when you're off work?'

What would you do if I didn't answer? I want to ask him.

'Do you want to stay in and watch a film with me this evening?'

For fuck's sake, when was the last time you were exciting? I want to say to him.

Would you completely grind to a halt if I never came back again? Would you weep? Would your life be over? Would your life begin? Come on, what would you do? 'Do you love me?' you ask. I love your love, but no, I don't love you. Sorry, but that's life. Is life supposed to be like this? Is this all love can offer? If it is, well then I simply don't understand it.

Have I made a mistake?
    Fuck, fuck.
    'I'll fry some steaks.'
    'I'll find you in town when you're off work.'
    'You bet.'
    'Yes, I love you.'
    Shit.

Plan:
    Live together.

Walk over to the co-op in sleet when I'm off work. Fried steak, soda water and fruit, oh, did you remember our membership card, back home in a stinking bus filled with people who smile and greet you, *iggu*, baby, you're ever so sweet, he says, my lips smile, my brain's about to explode;

another part of my mind says stop smiling, you ugly son of a bitch; can't stop thinking that I'm looking forward to going to bed this evening, disappearing into another world, waking up to the same shitty day tomorrow, hope he won't try to have sex with me, but I think it's likely, what reason should I come up with, let's go out, ouch, I've had a headache since this morning, feel like going to bed early this evening, *iggu*, I'll take care of you, put my arms around you, fucking hope he'll have something to do and want to go to bed late, wish he would at least play a video game but no, he's a gentleman, wish that some other woman had him, but no, he doesn't even look when a girl with a great ass passes by, that gentleman, fucking gentleman, *iggu*, you seem tired, were you busy today, you needn't begin all your sentences with *iggu*, yeah, been ever so busy; a true man that I will have to spend the rest of my life with, a man who chooses to take care of me instead of looking at a great ass, wish he'd look at an ass which isn't mine, *iggu*, don't worry, I'll make some food for you, I knew he'd say that, I can make my own food, you can hang out with your friends, isn't there football on, *iggu*, no, I'll take care of you when you're under the weather, I give up and nod, I'm already tired of him after forty-five minutes, need to be alone and light a cig before going indoors, *iggu*, smoking kills, is he joking, ha ha ha, how funny, kill me already, it's best if you suck in, smoke the cig until it's completely finished, he thinks that smoke smells so I don't wash my hands and ignore my bad breath, a gentleman who never grumbles, *iggu*, get some rest, life would be a bit more exciting if only he'd grumble a bit more,

I walk over to him, kiss me, he kisses me and gives me a
hug, *iggu*, I hope you'll feel better, I give up and go into my
room, log on to Facebook, would like to tag Peter and write:
does anyone want this man who never grumbles and never
glances at anybody else, I'm tired of my life, my back hurts
because I always sit hunched over, he loves me so much that
I want something evil to take possession of my body so that
I can knife him, four years in prison, rehabilitation, a new
life, maybe a more exciting life, and my boyfriend, future
husband, love him till death do us part, *iggu*, the food's just
about ready, *iggu iggu iggu* . . .

You better run for your fucking life or maybe I'll knife
myself, a gravestone with my name on it, date of birth, date
of death; you were already so dead that you might as well die
young; I'd be remembered as that woman who represents
everything that's evil, mothers would tell their children not
to follow in her footsteps, and I'd be useful that way, fuck
yes, I would, I'd laugh from down below and tell myself
that you fucking well deserve it, you triggered it because of
your self-pity and say *iggu*, *iggu*, *iggu* to myself, tormenting
my buried body so that I can teach myself a lesson, *iggu*,
come, dinner's ready, the devil's brought me back to earth,
punishing me before my reverie becomes too good, must
refrain from laughing, sit down at table, yum it tastes good,
iggu, please eat, there're lots of vitamins in the veggies, I
sigh, no longer listening to what he says, merely nodding,
he asks me something, didn't quite catch it, your colleagues
what, the sweetest man knows I'm not listening, but tries
again: *iggu*, have you seen Jørgen's work, no, why, *iggu*, it's

really inspiring, nod once more, you're really feeling bad today huh, feel the urge to leave, no, I just need some fresh air, I'll just go for a walk, *iggu*, yes, sounds like a good idea, I'll come with you, I could do with a breath of fresh air myself, crap, instant regret, *iggu*, put some warm clothes on, I'm not a baby I want to say, stop talking to me like that, but as he takes my hand, I take his hand, as he gives me his heart, I hold it, as he sacrifices his heart, I want to ruin it, it's almost bedtime, having just about survived yet another day, have enough strength, I can manage, I'll feel much better once I've slept, can survive yet another day if I dream of life tonight, maybe there's new life tomorrow, maybe another life entirely, maybe not, maybe yet another day like today, probably, hope's pointless, hope's dead, the gravestone reads: 'Hope, as you didn't show, I discovered that you weren't among us any more', now we're almost back home again. Something doesn't feel right, it has never felt right. Fresh air didn't do me any good, I've become wet, not in my pussy but because of rain and sleet, my pussy's dry, I fucking well hope he won't try this evening, *iggu*, what would you like to do when we're back home, as he winks at me I realise that hope really has passed away, am simply so tired that I go to bed, *iggu*, don't worry, I'll give you a massage, all right then, I brush my teeth and go to bed wide awake, he gives me a massage, feeling a bit better, thanks a lot, my sweetheart, I'm feeling better now, and before I've finished my sentence he places himself on top of me, fuck it, something hard touches my body, I love your body so much, I want you, I kiss him, no, I'm really exhausted, how about early tomorrow morning, *iggu*, okay then, he gives in because he's a gentleman but now he's slightly sad, *iggu*, I love you my darling, I love you but I'm just not in the mood because I'm so tired, he smiles because he's heard what he wants to hear, *iggu*, that's fine, let me put my arms around you till you fall asleep, and he holds me in his arms until I fall asleep, the sweetest man, my thoughts are elsewhere, I wonder how I can live such a life, I'm dead after all, how on earth can I treat the sweetest man so badly, what am I to do, oh well, I'll just have to try to sleep, after all there are no answers to my questions and yet another day, the very same day is about to dawn, and I must worship this holy night. Hope: you must rest in peace, what a shame that you've killed yourself.

Plan:
  Dead.

Death has begun to appear in my dreams, and I'm petrified. Murder. Death of the soul. A shrivelled corpse. Suicide. Death has begun to visit me, and I'm petrified. Mass murder. A failed suicide attempt. Envious of the dead. I've begun to walk hand in hand with it, and I'm petrified. I make up my mind because death won't leave my mind. There has always been something missing here.

'Anybody home?'
  'Hi.'
  '*Iggu*, sorry I'm late, I've been so busy,' he says.

'Peter, we need to talk.'

'Why have you packed your things?'

And then something like: what's going on, are you okay, are you leaving, what will you do, are you leaving me, et cetera, et cetera, et cetera, and I'm like: now listen to me, let's sit down and talk, I love you, I'm not happy, you're not happy, something's missing in my life, although we don't lack anything, I need to be on my own because we're not happy, et cetera and then the drama begins: are you not comfortable, why don't you want to be with me, what have I done, have I hurt you in any way, have I been stupid, and then golden words like: no, I'm tired of being comfortable, you've done nothing, I want to take care of myself, want to find myself, me, me, *me* and never *you*, it's not you, it never is you and so on, and the most predictable: have you found somebody else, don't you love me any more, don't you love me, don't you like me, don't you care for me at all, and then trying not to lose control: you know I love you very much, I *do* love you very much, but it's over, there's nothing to be done, so you must get it into your head, you must accept it, this is my final decision, this is final, *basta*, are you really leaving me, are you really not coming back to me, are we really splitting up, are you leaving, are you honestly leaving me, and on it goes, yes, yes, yes, are you leaving me, I'm leaving you, will you come back, I won't be coming back, are you leaving me, yes, I'm leaving you and you know the fucking rest but I'll tell you anyway.

Got to read his own fucking version of how to understand

the five fucking stages of loss, in endless text messages. Couldn't stop thinking of him, probably because he called every five fucking minutes. Had the fucking privilege of wiping his tears in the middle of the night, five fucking nights, to be exact. It was an honour to hold your heart, but my hands are all bloody, so you'd better take it or I'm gonna have to drop this sticky heart of yours. 'It's over' were my final words.

Then, just like that, I was free.

But the word 'free' didn't bring with it 'relief'. I was his future, after all.

*

'Come on, come out with me. It's been three weeks! Peter'll be okay!' Arnaq's growing tired of me and I'll have to go to this party at the university. I feel sorry for Peter, sitting at home all by himself, but I risk irritating the person I'm crashing with if I don't go, so I'm getting ready to join in with the night out.

'I really hope I don't bump into Peter,' I say to Arnaq.

'Are you coming? Yes! Yes! Yes!'

She begins to dance up against me, jokingly. I push her gently.

'It'll be fun! You won't regret it,' she says.

'Arnaq . . .'

'What? I just want to get wasted with you. It's been a long time!'

'I'm not drinking.'

'Come on . . .'

'Arnaq.'

'Yeah, yeah. Fine. Just come.'

'Let's wait and see,' I say.

'Honestly, get a life!'

'Are you trying to say that life's just about getting wasted and partying?' I joked.

'Yes, you'll see! There'll be guys – you know?'

She dangles a hairbrush in front of her crotch, pretending it's a dick.

'*Naamik* – no, no way. I'm finished with guys.'

'There are women, too, if you're off men . . . '

'Arnaq, you're an idiot. You're such a perv!'

Arnaq laughs loudly, and I laugh a bit too while I'm getting ready to go. Crazy girl.

When we get to Ilimmarfik, the University of Greenland, I go to the toilet with Arnaq, who wants to check her reflection one last time. I look at her while she's doing her face.

'Shit, you're ridiculously pale!' she says, surprised.

'That's okay.'

'Come over here.'

'Arnaq, it's okay.'

She walks over to me, puts some blusher on my cheeks although I don't really want her to.

'That's it!'

'Come on, let's join them.'

We leave the toilets, walk past the lift and the sofas and into the room.

'We're here!' shouts Arnaq.

I look like a servant trailing behind Arnaq who is a fucking queen and I only say hello to the people I know. Two of our fellow students are delighted to see us, immediately fetching some chairs and making room for us at the table. I try to sit next to Arnaq because I'm not in the mood to chat with people I don't know. Arnaq clutches her beer because she hasn't had a drink for a whole week. I take out my phone to check the time: 21.49. It's going to be a long night. I open my Coke. And at that very moment, at precisely this point in time, my lungs begin to breathe in air once again.

'Is there something in it?'

I discover that somebody's talking to me and I look up. For a moment, I'm absolutely floored.

'I'm sorry?'

'Is there something in it?' she tries once more.

'In what?'

'In your drink.'

'Something in it? What d'you mean?' I ask, confused.

'Just joking,' she says, awkwardly.

I look down quickly. Is there something in it? What? Oh! If it's spiked . . . No, no. Breathe in, breathe out. Calm down, I say to myself. It's okay. Oh no, I've been hit. Am horrified and mumble to Arnaq that I'm going out to smoke. Am so fucking confused that I might just as well be drunk. Light a cig and breathe in the lovely fragrance of spring. It can't be. It just can't be. I have to go home. I want to go home to Peter. And I hear the door open.

'What an amazing smell out here!' she says.

'What? The air?'

'No, your cig. But spring as well,' she answers.

I manage an awkward laugh.

'Sara,' she says.

'Who?'

'Sara. Me.'

'Oh, I just thought ... '

Don't know what to say so I shut up.

'What about you?' she asks.

'What?'

'What's your name?' she says, laughing a bit.

'Fia.'

'Hi Fia.'

'Hi Sara.'

I look down. Am embarrassed. I look so stupid that I decide to tell her I've got a lot on my mind right now so I'm easily confused. But something comes out of my mouth that I didn't plan. I lose control quickly.

'You're just so gorgeous that I can't get the words out.'

WHAT?

'What?' she asks, somewhat surprised.

'You're so beautiful.'

Where did that come from?

'Thanks,' she answers, puzzled but smiling.

'I ... '

I'm unable to talk any longer, point towards the door and walk back in.

She hasn't got anything to say herself, but merely nods as I walk away.

I walk to the toilet to try to calm myself down. What's going on? Did I, the most talkative person in the whole universe, fall silent? Am I, the world's best liar, not even able to tell a lie? That just can't be true. The comfort zone, which I've been trying to flee for three years, has just vanished. I'm excited. Frightened. I'm not comfortable and at ease. Peter. I want to find peace with Peter. I leave the toilet and my uncontrollable body walks itself back towards the sofa where Sara is. I can't stay away. Sit down with my head bent while I look in her direction because I can't stop myself. From Greenland to Africa, from Africa to the moon, from the moon to Venus, from Venus to the sun, from the sun to infinity, and from infinity back to here. She's more beautiful than this total distance. If God's a woman, then she's more beautiful than God. Sara. I could use some of Arnaq's vodka. Why haven't I seen her before? Who is she? I want to talk to her, ask her about everything. Want to ask where she suddenly came from. But I can't ask her, I've only just met her!

'Where did you suddenly come from?'

I can't control myself.

'I live in Nuussuaq. My friend invited me to the party.'

'How come we've never met before?' I ask her, pretty directly really.

'I think I've seen you on the bus before,' she says with a funny little smile.

'Really? When?'

She remembers me!

'Don't know. Don't remember. But if it was you, I think you were with your boyfriend.'

'My boyfriend? Peter? We split up. A little while ago. Because I don't love him.'

She nods with a smile because what on earth else can she do? I've only just met her; I must act more normal or she'll think I'm a bit insane. Why can't I tell a lie? Why can't I control my tongue? Why can't I simply just shut up? Did I smoke something inadvertently? Not possible, surely. This must be what it feels like to be high on drugs!

'Don't you want a drink?' she asks. Since she obviously wants to talk to me. Or maybe she's just being friendly because she thinks I'm crazy?

'I'm not really in the mood right now,' I answer.

'Me neither.'

'Same here,' I say.

Crap, I've just agreed with myself. Stupid. That's okay. Fia, you can do this. Breathe in ... I'm trying to say something so that she won't run away screaming. I try to stop staring at her, but in vain. She looks me in the eye. She smiles. What is she doing? Is she flirting? I send her a broad smile. My insides are burning and I feel my face flush. She notices it and smiles once more. Ouch, my heart.

'Need to work tomorrow, I don't think I'll go into town this evening,' she says.

'No way am I going into town. I'm not in the mood for men,' I say.

'Why are you talking about men?'

'They're boring. Only I'm not bored right now.'

'I'm not a man, am I!' she says, teasingly.

'I know that. I know that perfectly well. You're a woman. You look every inch a woman.'

'Thank you, I guess.'

'No, yes. You look like a woman; you're very attractive. That's what I mean,' I try to explain.

She bends her head and smiles.

We simply steal a glance at one another, smile and talk with other people for a while. I chat with Arnaq but haven't a clue what we're talking about because my thoughts are all over the place. I don't grasp Arnaq's story at all and glance over once again at the most beautiful woman in the whole world. She looks back at me and I want to scream, jump and throw my arms around her. I clench my fists. Ugh, I want to kiss her. Want to tell her that I want to kiss her. I'll never be able to find peace if I don't do it. Wh ... WHAT? My own thoughts frighten me. I don't want to kiss her! What am I thinking of? I know my boundaries. My boundary stops here. Why the hell would I want to kiss a woman? *Listen, you're not into women!* I tell myself. My body's simply confused as hell because of the recent changes in my life. I've only just begun to wake up after three years of hibernation. Yeah, I'm just confused. I have to leave. I'll go and hook up with a guy in town. I've been horny and unsatisfied for three years. Am pretty sure that this strange incident will evaporate and I look at her once more. She gives me a smile and I'm just about to tell her that I want to kiss her but instead I grab the chance to take my coat and go out to smoke. I come to my senses, for the first time since I saw her, when I fill my lungs with air and control my breathing. I feel excitement in my body. Looking forward to going into town, so that whatever has taken over my body can disappear. I'll hook up with a guy who I can take home with me so that I'm no longer turned on. After all I'm only an ordinary human being, who needs to be touched. Physically. That's all. I sense that Sara's on her way out when the door is opened. I know already what I want to say as I turn towards her.

'Are you okay?' she asks.

I nod and avoid eye contact.

'I'll be on my way home soon. I don't want to be tired at work tomorrow.'

'Think I'll head into town after all,' I answer.

'Thought you were off men?' she asks with a slight laugh.

'Yeah, I kind of am. But don't get me wrong. I'm not into women.'

She looks at me for a few seconds and then smiles.

'Don't get me wrong either. I'm not making a pass at you,' she says.

My whole body cringes as she says this. She doesn't like women. What should I do?

'Aren't you attracted to women?' I ask her very quickly.

'Yes, but I've got a girlfriend.'

I'm enormously relieved and let out a deep sigh. I just nod and walk in. I walk back to the living room and see that everybody's getting ready to leave. Although I'm disappointed at having to say goodbye to Sara, all I can do is get ready to leave with them. While we're waiting for taxis, I stand outside the crowd in the hope that Sara will come over to me. She doesn't. I go back, embarrassed. Stupid. Muster the strength to look at her as the fucking taxis, which come between us, arrive and everybody's busy getting into them. Finally I look in the direction of sweet Sara to say goodbye and discover that she's already far away. Feel a sense of loss inside. Since there's nothing else to do, I get into a taxi and look back at the crowd until I lose sight of the scene. That fucking taxi driver is going too fucking fast. We disappear behind something. I've vanished. An unknown feeling engulfs me – it calls itself Love. Love? Oh, come on. You haven't met Love. This isn't Love. It's not Love. THIS ISN'T LOVE. Give me a break, for heaven's sake.

Town is pretty fucking grim, and I fill my soul with alcohol as quickly as I can. Oh my God. What the fuck am I going to do? What the fuck am I supposed to do? Okay.

'Arnaq, please buy two shots of Fisherman for me as well.'

'Sure,' she shouts.

When she comes back, I drink the two shots in one go and tolerate some pig who's trying to chat me up. What's his name? Albert? Johannes? Anton? Nikolaj? Sausage! Sausage? Oh, well, it doesn't matter. Who he is doesn't matter. A dick is a dick. I turn towards him, close my eyes and return his kisses. His beard scratches my face, making my skin itch. His lips are dry. Fuck it. I turn away from him. Arnaq sees us and is exceedingly proud of her victory.

'Your Fucking Highness, may your will be served!' I shout at her.

She toasts me with a laugh.

I'm doing it to forget Sara, I whisper so that nobody can hear it.

It's Sara. Sara. Ah, the ice inside me melts. I begin to kiss Pig-With-A-Nose-Like-A-Prick again. I see that the bar's lights have come on. Can't be bothered to listen to Her Fucking Highness's fucking speech and hurry and grab Wild-Boar-What's-His-Fucking-Name's hand and follow him out. I drag him to the nearest taxi, avoiding looking at him while he silently feels me up. As soon as we're home, he begins to tear the clothes off me although he's got no idea where my room is. He's a freaking animal. I might be, too, but he's an ugly one. I might be, too, but I'm pretty sure sausages taste worse. No choice but to allow him as I point, irritated, towards the room I'm staying in. He doesn't even bother with foreplay, hasn't noticed that I'm not turned on. He proudly shows me his fucking sausage. Is that something to be proud of? I think to myself. There's really nothing good to say about what comes next, and because he's so drunk I don't even bother to fake an orgasm. When the few minutes, which feel like an eternity, are over and he's done, he throws his heavy body over mine. I push it away. He keeps trying to kiss me so I take my clothes and walk out to the bathroom. My reflection is so ugly that I touch my face to make it look better but then I remember the man in my room, so I let my fucked-up hairstyle and the remnants of my makeup stay as they are so that he can flee in horror. He's just human. Just a man. A man with a sausage in his pants. Remember, just a sausage. I let out a deep sigh and walk in to the man with the sausage. I lie down and discover that he's hard again, so I snatch my phone and I try to look surprised.

'Oh no, my parents are on their way home!' I shout.

'It's Arnaq's apartment,' he says.

He's obviously sobered up.

'No, my parents live here.'

'I had a thing with Arnaq. I know perfectly well what her apartment looks like.'

'Don't you know that Arnaq's my mother?'

I know that he knows I'm making fun of him, but even so I throw his clothes at him still with a serious expression on my face.

'Hurry up. I have to puke!' His sausage has shrunk so much that it's no longer alarming, just pathetic. I laugh. I can't be bothered with him so I decide to fuck with him. I begin to pretend that I'm about to throw up.

'I'm really going to puke!'

I run over to him for help.

'Go to the toilet, for fuck's sake!'

He pushes me towards the bathroom.

I go inside and lock the door while I exaggerate with loud sounds to make him believe that I'm being sick. After a few minutes, I hear him leave the apartment very quietly. I smile. Mission accomplished. Now I can sleep and forget everything.

The sunlight through the window has made everything hot and I kick my duvet off my sweaty body. I smell my hangover breath, which reminds me of yesterday's awful events and I feel a strong urge to take a bath. The memory of the sausage man makes me nauseous and I remember my legendary throwing-up act and laugh, which actually makes me cough something up. I hurry out into the kitchen and chug an entire bottle of Coke and do everything I can to keep it down. Last night has really taken its toll. I sit down on the sofa and crunch some leftover crisps while I wonder why Arnaq still hasn't come home. It's a shame that she drinks so much all the time since she lost her job. My little brother is best friends with her, and I really hope she won't be a bad influence. Arnaq's a woman, an *arnaq* – the very word for woman – with a mind of her own, who's never boring and here I am, waiting for her to come home with new stories. I have a wish. I want Arnaq to have hooked up with another woman, to turn up with a gay morning-after story. But of course, Arnaq's a woman with a mind of her own, and sometimes I envy her laid-back lifestyle. If Arnaq, who can easily hook up with another *arnaq*, has hooked up with a man, then I can't be bothered to hear about it. I'm suddenly dying to know. I yearn for excitement.

Just as I'm losing patience, I hear somebody trying to open the door and I hurry over. A rather intoxicated Arnaq enters the room as if she's fucking royalty and I laugh at her.

'What's up, Arnaq? Did you sleep at all?'

'The night is still young. I'll sleep when I die!' she says cheekily, stripping off her coat.

'Where've you been?' I ask, hopefully.

'Not telling!'

'Did you go home with someone?'

I follow her into the living room.

She sits down on the sofa and refuses to say anything. Gives me a playful smile.

'Woman? Man?'

'Does that matter?' she asks, slightly irritated.

I know that she doesn't like to be quizzed like this but I'm too curious to give up.

'No, it's irrelevant. I just want to know because you tell such great stories.'

'What about you? Did you bring Kristian home with you? You should be the first one to spill,' she says.

'Who's Kristian?'

'Oh, come on! Were you that drunk? Kristian!'

The sausage man's name is Kristian, apparently. If I'm going to get her story, I'll have to tell her about my horror show.

'I brought him home with me,' I say with a laugh.

'Honestly? Here? Surely you know, don't you, that I had a thing with him? Yep, that manwhore!'

She roars with laughter.

'He remembered. He totally knew this was your place. He said so.'

'Shit, how embarrassing!' she says and begins to laugh uncontrollably.

'What about you? Who did you hook up with?' I ask.

'You can't tell anybody else!'

'Who would I tell? I promise I won't.'

'Inaluk.'

'Inaluk who?' I ask.

'Inaluk Inaluk.'

'*Inaluk?*' Now this is a surprise.

She nods.

'Is she gay? I thought she had a guy?'

'Please don't tell anybody!'

'I'll keep quiet. Don't worry.'

'I think it was the first time she was with a woman,' she says, slightly embarrassed.

'Oof. Was she bad?'

'No, but she was a bit hesitant.'

'How do women do it?' I ask Arnaq, without thinking.

'Can't you figure it out? God, you have no imagination!'

She gets up from the sofa and walks over to her room.

'Arnaq . . . I was just asking.'

'Then come here. You can't know until you've tried it! LET'S SCREW!' she jokes from her room.

What would it be like, how would she react, if I did come, what would it be like to try with her, what might it do to our friendship, what would she look like naked, would she not look sexy, how would she kiss, how would she screw, what would it be like, how could I go in there? I couldn't. I wouldn't dream of it. My thoughts make no sense. I'm simply tired of sausages. Believe me, I've tried all sorts of sausages. Cocktail sausages, frankfurters, red, brown, yellowish, big, small, sausages . . . you name it. I'm sick of them. I'm off sausages. I want to take a bath, scrub my body clean so that the stench of sausage can vanish without leaving a trace in the water pipes.

Plan:
  No more sausage.

Friday once again. It's a strange week for me. I haven't been to classes and I need to get out a bit. I decide to switch off the computer although I keep thinking of stuff I've found on the Internet. Romantic attraction, sexual attraction or sexual behaviour between members of the same sex or gender. Google knows everything. But I still haven't found the answer. Doubt, ignorance and confusion make me restless. But even so, I don't want to go back to my comfort zone. My comfort zone is gone. I've recovered from that fucking travesty last Friday, and Arnaq and I have decided to deal with our restlessness. Hope has returned from the dead, popping up like the devil. All I need is to see her briefly. Because I need to get to grips with my desperate brain.

'What have you bought?' I ask Arnaq as she walks in.
  'A bottle of vodka and some mixers,' she answers in a breezy voice.
  'A whole bottle? That'll kill us!'
  'What did you get?' she says.
  'Four beers.'
  'Four beers? I'll teach you how to party!' she laughs.
  Maybe she thinks she should be proud of herself for always being shitfaced. I know I don't want to get drunk

and I will prove it. She's fucking well not going to drag *me* down with her.

'Four shots of vodka!' I shout through a crowd of people to the bartender.

'Four?' asks Arnaq happily.

'It's on me!'

Because I haven't seen hope yet. I want to escape that horrible disappointment. I want to get shitfaced! I want to party till I'm invincible! But things are looking up as my favourite song comes on in the bar: 'Crimson and Clover' by Joan Jett and the Blackhearts.

'Arnaq, where will the after-party be when it closes?'

She isn't listening to me. Maybe she's fucking delirious.

Fucking delirious.

'Fia! Did I tell you I was crazy about a woman? Do you remember that?'

I nod.

'Don't look now! There's a woman with short hair right behind you. It's *her*!'

I turn my head slowly. Am excited to see a lesbian but immediately disappointed at what I see. Apart from her beautiful face, she has the body of a man. Without the sausage.

'Wouldn't it just be the same as being with a man?' I ask her jokingly.

'Oh fuck, but she's so sweet! I'd marry her if she didn't have a girlfriend.'

'Has she got a girlfriend?' I ask.

'Ugh, yes. She's here. She's coming over,' she says, surprised.

I turn my head calmly so that nobody notices. Sara. Then I grind to a halt. I'm now running on hope.

I admit it: for the first time in my life I'm feeling something very powerful. I don't think I can escape it. I'm about to enter new territory and I'm horrified. I'm about to cross the line but I can't stop. What is it I feel? Lust. How do you say lust in Greenlandic? It's risky. It's *very* risky. I just can't stop until I get what I want, I don't *want* to give up. It's *that* taboo. My body's struggling to survive, and I'm fighting to breathe because I'm being smothered. I can feel my lungs fighting to keep up. I want her. I'll go mad if I don't have her. Lust. My pulse rises. My blood begins to flow again. After three years, arisen from the dead, ascended into heaven. Or down? I don't give a shit. I've come alive! Jesus, welcome back to life!

'Hi,' says Sara, brushing my back with her hand. Suddenly I can't figure out what to say and give her a broad smile instead. I want so much to kiss her that I can hardly control myself. 'Crimson and Clover' is still playing in the background, giving us the perfect soundtrack.

'Are things okay with you?' I think she asks me.

'Yes, I'm fine. How about you?'

Am positively surprised at my answer and feel safe.

'Fine, thanks,' she answers. 'Nice meeting you the other day.'

'Same here. It's nice to see you,' I hear my heart say.

She smiles and seems charmed by my reply but then straightens her back when she sees Arnaq next to me.

'We were on our way home. See you again soon,' she says.

No, fuck no, please don't leave me, stay by my side, don't go away. Let me touch you, let me kiss you, let me take you home to my place, no fucking way, no, don't disappear, you'll smash me into a million pieces if you disappear, you'll knock me down just when I've finally stood up, you're killing me now that I've come alive again, please, oh God please, don't leave me again.

'Where are you off to?' I hear myself say, but the person I'm talking to doesn't hear me. She's left me. My survival instinct kicks in. Need to survive. I feel the need. The need to survive. I turn towards Arnaq.

'Fia, did you hook up with Sara?' she asks me, covering her mouth.

I remain silent as she begins to stare at me and I can no longer keep my secret.

'No, we haven't been together ...'

'Since when have you been attracted to women? Wh– what's going on?' she stutters and laughs.

I feel the need. 'How about we get out of here?'

She gives me a confused look. I look her in the eye. She's no longer confused. She's turned on. Feels the need too.

Through a crowd of people, making a beeline for a taxi, towards Qinngorput, a new area of Nuuk, our hands touching, my heart's racing, it hurts, sexual attraction, animal behaviour, survival, silence on the way in, awkward opening the door, have you brought your keys, she passes me, touching my body with hers. She's willing, she's hot, thinks I'm hot too, don't know what I am but I am drunk, 'Let's go to my room,' she says gently, puts me down on her bed, can hardly, don't know how I'm to begin, thank goodness for Arnaq, she calls the shots, strips off in front of me, her stomach, bra, thighs, new sight, dark sensation, my body says it's right, my brain's in doubt, she's coming closer, climbs on top of me, 'Do you really want to?' she asks, 'Is it okay?' I ask, she comes closer, her breathing is getting heavier, what I see is beautiful, fragile, want to touch but am unable to, tremble, she's my friend, don't want my friend but her body, I want another woman, but I replace her with Arnaq, an *arnaq*, my thoughts are moving fast, time stands still, her lips touch, first my neck then my lips, she has no beard, doesn't sting, she's soft, lovely, but she's Arnaq and not Sara, but that's okay because she's an *arnaq*, a woman, everything moves inside me, remember now that this is how it feels down below, it tickles, I look up at Arnaq, can hardly believe, 'Are you wet?' she asks, I say 'Yes' and ask her whether it's okay, 'It's okay, you just follow me,' she says, can no longer recognise the Arnaq I know, kiss Arnaq, the hot girl, kiss the holy *arnaq* again, the holy woman, our hands take off clothes, our bodies, our skin, touch each other, her hand brushes, reaches where, the next thing is what I fear, but I move my hand, am able to because it's not Peter, reach the place, discover that it's not a sausage, I confirm because it's not a sausage, I confirm that I like it, have found my answer.

I wake up relieved that Arnaq isn't there and hurry into my bedroom. I don't know what to feel about last night's revelation. Strange that it was Arnaq. Yet not strange that it was a woman.

I'm scared of last night's revelation. My dream of getting out of my comfort zone has been fulfilled, and I have no idea what to do. Last night answered many of my questions, and my heart aches in a way I've never known before. I confirm what I can't get out of my mind. I'll have to tell Sara. I'm suffering. But I'd rather feel pain than not feel anything. I take a piece of paper and start writing; what I feel, the things I want to do to her, how sweet she is . . . The words come to me from the song – our song – 'Crimson and Clover'.

*

Sara. One woman. Two weeks of fantasies. Thousands of unspoken words. Millions of questions. Thoughts and emotions that rush towards infinity. Hours slowing down. My numb self can feel again. My fantasies become stronger. I no longer doubt my existence. Only I haven't seen her again. The spring night is bright, quiet. Now and then some drunk people pass by. Have been lying in my bed for hours and I don't think I can fall asleep. All of this has blown me wide open and I have to tell somebody. I begin to long for my little brother. I ignore the time and give him a call as he's always supportive.

'Hi,' he says.

He's with a crowd of people by the sound of it.

'Hi, am I disturbing you?' I ask him in a voice that is loud but a bit croaky because I haven't spoken all day.

'No, wait a moment. I'll go outside.'

'That's okay. I'll call you back tomorrow.'

'No, I've just gone out. Are you okay?' he says. It's quieter now.

'I'm fine. I just miss you.'

Just listening to his voice makes me almost burst into tears.

'I miss you too. It's good to hear from you. I really want to see you.'

'What are you doing?'

'We're at an after-party. My friend invited me yesterday evening, and we went into town.'

'Hope it's fun.'

Don't know what else to do so I start to say goodbye.

'Come and join me,' he says enthusiastically. 'I'll pay for the taxi.'

Find the thought of drinking off-putting but accept the invitation so that I can get out. I'll only fester if I stay here.

I arrive in a taxi and see that my brother's waiting to pay my fare. The strange feeling inside me fades as I give him a hug, and I'm ready to tell him what's happened. It's about time. The first step. My life will change, I can feel it. We enter one of the many blocks of flats, and on the staircase I already smell cigarette smoke and hear music and laughter. I feel awkward because I'm not drunk but am comfortable with my brother, who's standing next to me. We walk towards the living room and pass some drunken people. We meet a crowd of young people sitting on sofas, and I look around for someone I might recognise.

It really *was* love at first sight. I'm now absolutely sure that she sees me. It's true that I've met Love. I see that she knows it too when her eyes meet mine. I acknowledge that she has also acknowledged it when she walks over to me and gives me a smile. I fetch the paper out of my pocket and give it to her. Because words can't explain or describe. I give her my heart. She reads it, looks me straight in the eye, moves away from me, and my heart stops. Sara, you've won my heart ... And she picks up a guitar. We look at one another among dancing bodies. Sara; my heart ... Sara, my heart.

She sings. Our song. Which is precisely when my heart begins again. Beats once more. It was *meant* to be. It was meant to be you. It was meant to be me and you. She walks over to me, and my world is totally silent. I only look at her, and the sensation within me is infinite. She takes hold of me and escorts me out of the door, and I don't resist. The spring night is invigorating. Nature has quietly come to life again, and that's all I hear. There's something beautiful in front of me. From Greenland to infinity, and back again ... What a day to be alive. She reads the note I have been carrying around for two weeks. The spring night gives me life, and Sara kisses me. What a day to realise I'm not dead. Love has rescued me. And I realise that this is my coming-out story.

'Crimson and Clover,' she says.

'Over and over,' I reply.

INUK

1 May

I've arrived at the prison. The walls, which I thought were low when I saw them from above, fence in the area like tall mountains. I discover that it's impossible to escape. I recognise the distinctive smell and the feeling of suffering. I also discover that time hasn't changed anything. I meet withdrawn inmates and lose all the strength I had mustered. I realise that I shouldn't be here at all and that I'll have to flee. But since you can't just run away from an enormous prison, I need to draw up a plan. Because I have to escape and never come back. I look at the inmates that I'll be living with. I can tell they're so institutionalised that they stare at one another till they start to lose their minds. It frightens me. They stare at me and wait. They look at me like a pack of animals, ready to bite. They want to infect me, make me a mad dog too. Their eyes show that they're desperate to see me suffer and they'll laugh at me when, in anguish, I struggle to survive. A single mistake and I'm dead. If I'm going to make it, I need to sacrifice something. I sacrifice my soul.

Inuk

24 May

Today is the day. Today's escape attempt just *has* to be successful. The prison makes me want to puke. There's an acidy smell in the halls because the inmates have begun to putrefy. They stink so bad that I feel quite sick. The mould has scarred my skin and caused swellings all over my body. I'm so nervous that I no longer register the stench from my armpits, which usually gives me a headache. I need air. Perhaps the inmates know because they are staring at me with more interest. I *have* to escape now. If not, they'll humiliate me. If not, they'll abuse me until I'm powerless. If not, they'll rape me. When they've finished, they'll murder me. Today is the day. The day when I run. The day when I am born.

Inuk

25 May

The roads are unrecognisable. They don't fence you in like tall mountains. The human beings aren't inmates. Roads without walls replace the corridors. My lungs inhale unpolluted air. People here are wiser. They don't look at me. They aren't keeping an eye on me. They don't want to hurt me. They don't care about me. I breathe. I've escaped.

I HAVE ESCAPED.

Fugitive

My dear sister

Do you remember when I had a toothache while Mum and the others were out boating? Do you remember that we saw *Free Willy* and that I kept on falling asleep while you took care of me? I often wonder whether you felt responsible, whether you felt like a child or a grown-up when they left us alone. You've taken care of me ever since. I hope you're fine. I'm sorry that I just vanished. I was afraid that your concern might prevent me from carrying out my plans, and I hope that one day you'll understand. I'm in Copenhagen and I don't know for how long. I can only be reached via this PO box. You know I never felt at home in Greenland and I had to escape. Arnaq might have told you; if she hasn't, then don't believe what you hear because it isn't true. People have begun to talk shit because they have nothing else to talk about but they shouldn't be trusted. Please understand that I'm not running away from you. I don't want to talk about it right now; I only hope that despite the rumours you hear, you'll believe what I say. If you're tired of staying at Arnaq's then feel free to move in to my apartment. Here's the key. Don't try to take care of me, it's time for me to learn to take care of myself. I've got a place to stay. I'm so grateful to you for providing for me. If you think I'm making a mistake, just let me. You have to let me go. I'm sorry about our last meeting and what followed. I wish you the very best.

Inuk

1 June

Now that I'm away from the rotting mould, my swellings are beginning to heal. There's no longer any pus and the stinging areas are manageable. Sometimes, blood seeps out; it will stop soon. But it's not healing properly at all: my swellings have formed scars and they're very noticeable. People are beginning to see them. I loathe those scars, which I will have for the rest of my life and can't bear to look at. I'm ashamed of them. I'm scarred for life. But I got out before the mould took me. I'm grateful for having escaped.

Survivor

My dear little brother

I remember when I took care of you and you had a toothache. We would often watch *Free Willy* but it was *Beethoven*
we watched that evening and I remember that you cried. I
also remember when we watched the Kelly Family play in
their band on TV, and you wanted to have long hair like
them, but Mum would cut it every time because you were a
boy. You'd have been so cute if you had long hair. I remember that I felt responsible when I babysat you. I never felt like
a grown-up. I felt like an older sister. I was always so proud
of having such a sweet little brother like you. I'm still proud
of you and that will never change. Thank you for the key. I'll
take good care of your apartment till you're back. I haven't
really talked to Arnaq lately because we're both so busy.
What's happened? Your letter surprised me and I wish you
could tell me a bit more so that I can help. Don't apologise
at all for our last meeting. *I'm* the one who should say sorry.
There's so much I need to tell you – we need to sit down and
talk. I know that you can take care of yourself but I love you
so much I can't just pretend I'm not concerned. I'd feel so
much better if you would just give me a call. I want to hear
more about the incident you mentioned and to be allowed
to explain our last get-together. Please call me.

I love you so much. Take care.

Your big sister,

Fia

3 June

Today I went on Facebook because I couldn't stay away any longer. I was terrified of looking at my messages but I did it anyway.

Ivalo Løvstrøm:

You've told lies about my husband. I want you to admit publicly that what you said isn't true.

Arnaq:

I'm sorry.

Fia:

Where are you?

Little brother, I'm worried. Have you left?

Give me a call. Now.

The rumour is everywhere on my news feed. It's worse than I thought.

'OMG. Have you heard about Miki Løvstrøm? Maybe it's true?' 26 likes, 14 comments.

'People with double lives shouldn't be members of the Inatsisartut!' 31 likes, 3 comments.

'Our country is coming to a standstill! Our leaders are frauds.' 7 likes, 21 comments.

'Bloody queer.' 16 likes.

I wouldn't have survived if I hadn't escaped. But here they can't touch me. Never again will I return to Greenland. Never again will I be holed up in prison again. Never again will I be walled up behind tall mountains. Never again will

I call a Greenlander my fellow countryman. Never ever will I go back to live among the prison inmates. Because I'm ashamed to call myself a Greenlander.

Refugee

Dear Arnaq

I've thought of writing to you for a long time but couldn't find the words. But now I need a reply, which is why I'm writing to you. Please fill this out and send it back to me.

1. Do you feel better when you say something that gets everybody's attention? ☐ Yes ☐ Maybe
2. Do you like to hurt other people? ☐ Yes ☐ No
3. Do you think it's funny to make fools of others? ☐ Yes ☐ Maybe
4. Do you know what respect is? ☐ Yes ☐ No
5. Have you ever been in love? ☐ Yes ☐ No
6. If yes to question five, do you only love yourself? ☐ Yes ☐ No
7. If yes to question five, do you love your friends? ☐ Maybe ☐ No
8. Do you want to hurt them? ☐ Yes ☐ No
9. Do you have any emotions? ☐ Yes ☐ No
10. Did you feel anything when you broke my trust? ☐ Maybe ☐ No
11. Did you achieve something when you hurt me? ☐ Yes ☐ Maybe
12. Did you achieve what you wanted to when you ruined my life? ☐ Yes ☐ No
13. Do you have any regrets? ☐ Yes ☐ No
14. Do you think I'll forgive you? ☐ No
15. Are you a heartless bitch? ☐ Yes

Thank you in advance,
    Inuk

5 June

Are people happy?
  Are people scared?
  Are people satisfied?
  Are people like me?
  Are people scarred?
  Are people small?
  Are people curious?
  Are people horny?
  Are people high?
  Are people serious?
  Are people dead?
  Are people alive?

People don't care.
  THIS IS IT. PARADISE.
  High Jesus, sitting at God's right hand.

Dear Fia

Do you remember when I first discovered that you had started drinking and smoking? Do you remember how sad I was when I found out? I often wonder whether your bad friends influenced you or whether this was something you decided on your own. I often wonder whether you promised to quit so I wouldn't be disappointed or whether you just said it to comfort me. I've always wanted to deliver you from evil. I think we need to talk about the last time we saw each other. After you and Peter split and you moved in with Arnaq, in the space of a few weeks I could tell that you had changed a lot. I actually thought I knew you but I was very shocked when I saw you and Sara kiss. I accept that Arnaq has influenced you, I just need to know whether she is to blame for any of this. Because if she has affected you in some way, I need to stop her. I need to tell you about Arnaq. You can't trust her. She doesn't keep her promises. Although she may seem extremely charming on the outside, she's rotten inside. She'll happily smash someone else into thousands of pieces to get what she wants. She looks like an angel, but she's the devil personified. Trouble is, you can't see her fucking horns.

Arnaq in one word: evil.

I'll prove it if you don't believe me. Not so very long ago, she lied about me, simply in order to get what she wanted. Do you remember the night the three of us went to a party in Kujallerpaat Street? After you went home, Arnaq called me in the early hours and told me that she couldn't sleep.

She asked me whether she could come to our after-party, and I said sure. But as soon as she walked in the door, I could sense that something horrible was going to happen. In that early morning, I discovered what Arnaq was actually like. I had always thought that I could trust her and I told her something I'd experienced at work. You must have read about this guy, Miki Løvstrøm, from the Inatsisartut. He's an MP. Everybody is talking about him on Facebook, but don't believe it. I told her that although he had a wife and children, he had once tried to hook up with me, and she promised never ever to speak about it to anybody. Of course, you understand how important it was that this piece of information didn't get out. And now that people suspect Miki lives a double life and lies about it, everyone's going mad. Greenland isn't a good place to come out in public right now. Soon Miki will try to save himself by denying it through the media. You know how much power the Inatsisartut has. They don't make mistakes. This means that I'll be fired although I had nothing to do with it. Arnaq told my secret to a lot of people at the after-party. I honestly hoped that people would keep it quiet but I was naïve. Miki will deny everything until people stop talking. I'm just waiting to be fired and there's nothing I can do about it. I have no idea why Miki came on to me. I don't know what to do, I have no experience with this sort of thing. I haven't done anything. And because Arnaq is a fucking gossip queen, everyone has heard about it now. Her malicious story has spread and I'm left holding the baby. What I want you to know is this: Arnaq was fully aware of the possible consequences of her actions, and she betrayed me. She wants me to be the sinner. Now she's got me where she wants me and you're her next prey. All of this proves that queers are evil. They have some sort of mental illness and although they act like normal people, you can't ever let them out of your sight. They should get treatment. They're dangerous. They can't be trusted, and you have to be on your guard. You're not into women, I know that. You're okay. You're not evil. Arnaq has just dragged you down with her. You're so much better than that. I'm asking you to drop Arnaq and never go back. I don't want to lose you.

Inuk

12 June

Front page in sermitsiaq.ag:
MIKI LØVSTRØM: THIS IS SLANDER.
Knew this was coming.
Liar

Dear Inuk

I remember when I started drinking and smoking. I remember that it made you so unhappy. Although the difference in our ages isn't big, our lives were different in those days. When I started drinking and smoking, I wasn't influenced by bad friends, it was just something I did. It's part of being in your teens, isn't it? When I promised to stop I said it to comfort you. You were a child at the time and you didn't see it as I did, which you must understand. I'm sorry that I never tried to explain this to you.

I've heard the rumours about Miki Løvstrøm. You can't avoid them. I'm very cross that Arnaq has treated you like that. It hurts me to know that it hurts you. I know all about how Arnaq behaves but I'm surprised that she would behave like that towards a good friend. But *this* you must understand: I never had a close relationship with Arnaq while I lived at her place. I only crashed with her and we went on a few nights out together. We had fun but I noticed she had issues from the beginning and I've kept my distance. Now that she's betrayed you, it just confirms that her problems rule her life. I'm sorry that you're going through this. Inuk, I want to say sorry for the last night we saw each other. You shouldn't have discovered it the way you did. But you have to understand one thing: Arnaq hasn't done me any harm. She didn't drag me along. I wasn't under her influence. My and Sara's kiss didn't have anything to do with Arnaq. It's nobody's fault; I kissed Sara because I wanted to. Sorry, but believe me when I say that kissing Sara was *my* decision. A few weeks later, I fell in love. My love for her is still growing, and now I know that I'm gay. Inuk, I'm gay. You've always delivered me from evil but love isn't evil. I'm not evil. I sense your pain. I can understand your anger. But queers aren't to blame for all that's evil. Be angry at me, if you need to, but don't let your anger destroy you. I'm here if you need me. You'll understand one day, and I'm looking forward to that. I hope you'll open up. You can tell me anything and I'll stand by you. I'll never ever shatter the confidence you have in me, and you must never forget that. Whatever has happened, whatever will happen, please know that I'm here. I won't leave you. I'm not evil. I love you. My dear brother, I love you very much.

Fia

13 June

HOMOPHOBIC CLAUSTROPHOBE
  FUCKING QUEERS ARE SICK!
  FUCKING QUEERS ARE CONTAGIOUS!
  FUCKING QUEERS ARE FUCKING GREENLANDERS!
  FUCKING QUEERS ARE SUBHUMAN!
  FUCKING QUEERS MUST DIE!
  Claustrophobic Homophobe

Dear Fia

Do you remember when you didn't believe me when I said I was sick? I threw up right afterwards. Do you remember when you didn't believe me when I hurt myself? I turned black and blue right afterwards. Do you remember when you didn't believe me when I told you I missed you? I began to weep right afterwards. Do you remember when I told you to be careful and you didn't want to listen to me? You got into trouble right afterwards. Do you remember when I begged you not to leave me, and you did? You began to miss me right afterwards. You're wrong even if you're older than me. I'll always forgive you. I'll always love you because you're my sister. But you must believe *me* now. You must believe me. You're wrong. You're on an island that will never change. You're on an island with no way out. You're on an island from which you can't escape. You're on the completely wrong island. *Your* way of thinking is wrong. When you escape from the island, you'll realise that you were in the wrong place. When you escape from the island, you'll have no problem in choosing the right way to live. I want you to come now. I want you to believe me. Come now. Believe me. You'll regret it if you stay.

Inuk

Dear Inuk

I remember that you always forgave me when I made mistakes. I'm sorry. In those days, I wasn't aware of my mistakes. What I know now is that I haven't made a mistake. It's not a mistake to love. Forgive me. I'm waiting here for you, I'll always wait for you. I've already said it: I'll always be by your side.

   With love,
   Fia

20 June

The island has run out of oxygen. The island is swollen. The island is rotten. The island has taken my beloved from me. The island is a Greenlander. It's the fault of the Greenlander.

One who doesn't want to be a Greenlander

My dearest Inuk

I've filled these out:

Do you think I'll forgive you	☑ No
Are you a heartless bitch?	☑ Yes

Forgive me.
Arnaq

21 June

To be a Greenlander is explained in the following way:

You're a Greenlander when you were born and raised in Greenland.

You're a Greenlander when you help develop your country.

You're a Greenlander when you speak the language.

You're a Greenlander when you take an interest in its culture.

You're a Greenlander when you respect your ancestors.

You're a Greenlander when you love your country.

You're a Greenlander when you're proud of your nationality.

You're a Greenlander when you feel Greenlandic.

What it really means to be a Greenlander:

You're a Greenlander when you're an alcoholic.

You're a Greenlander when you beat your partner.

You're a Greenlander when you abuse children.

You're a Greenlander when you were neglected as a child.

You're a Greenlander when you feel self-pity.

You're a Greenlander when you suffer from self-loathing.

You're a Greenlander when you're full of anger.

You're a Greenlander when you're a liar.

You're a Greenlander when you're full of yourself.

You're a Greenlander when you're stupid.

You're a Greenlander when you're evil.

You're a Greenlander when you're queer.

Our nation, you who are ancient: go to the mountain and
never come back.

Stop being so fucking pompous.

And take your rotten children with you.

Greenlander by force

23 June

Front page in sermitsiaq.ag:

MIKI LØVSTRØM: THE MEDIA IS PERSECUTING AN INNOCENT MAN.

Silent

28 June

Greenland is not my home. I feel sorry for the Greenlanders. I'm ashamed of being a Greenlander. But I'm a Greenlander. I can't laugh with the Danes. I don't find them funny. I can't keep up a conversation with the Danes. I find it boring. I can't act like the Danes. I'm unable to imitate them. I can't share Danish values. I don't respect them. I'll never look like the Danes. I can't become blond or fair-skinned. I can't be a Dane among Danes. I'm not a Dane. I can't live in Denmark. Denmark is not my country.

Where is home?

If home isn't in Greenland, if home isn't here, where is my home?

Lost

Dear Arnaq

I received your reply. I don't think you're a bitch. Sorry for writing such harsh words; but you must understand the consequences of your actions. Do you remember what we promised each other? We promised that nothing could break apart our close friendship. We promised that it would always be the two of us. Our friendship was so strong that I opened up to you, and *only* you. You smashed what you said was unbreakable. Arnaq: I know your history. I know you're struggling with problems in your life. I know who you are. I know that my parents weren't alcoholics even though they grew up under Danish rule. I know that my parents weren't neglected as children. I know that I wasn't neglected the way you were. What you've experienced is awful; I'm aware of that. Your struggle is tough; I can well understand. But let me tell you this: you're responsible for your own actions. Believe me when I say I've been to hell and back, but I don't blame others when the fault is mine. I'm responsible for my own actions. Please understand me when I ask you to act like a grown-up. You're not a child. What I'm trying to say is this: when you failed your exam, you blamed it on the teacher. When you were fired from work, you said that our boss was incompetent. When you were caught with a man who was in a monogamous relationship, you said that it was purely his fault. When you became an alcoholic, you said it was in your DNA. When you had to explain your anger, you said that your dad had abused you. When you could no longer handle your life, you declared that your parents didn't love you. And you betrayed your friend's trust, using your personal problems as an excuse; you just can't cope with life. Stop feeling so sorry for yourself because there's no reason that you should be pitied. Enough of this post-colonial shit. It's your own fault if you regret your actions after betraying my confidence. It's your own fault that you're sad because you ruined our friendship. It's your own fault that after abusing my love, you're on your own. Karma is a bitch. But you're not to blame for the bad things in my life. I'm to blame for my own problems. It's *my* fault that I trusted you and told you my secret. It's my own fault that I sold my soul to the devil. If I were you, I'd keep my eyes open. Evil pops up when you least expect it. You know, what goes around comes around.

Inuk

30 June

Front page in sermitsiaq.ag

JOURNALIST FIRED AFTER BEING ACCUSED OF FABRICATING LØVSTRØM STORY.

Jobless

My dearest Inuk

I've understood every single word. I understand you. I'm
sorry. What can I do? Have I ruined everything?
  Arnaq

4 July

I hate that Greenlanders talk shit about each other all the time.

I hate that Greenlanders talk shit to each other all the time.

I hate that Greenlanders are so angry at each other.

I hate that Greenlanders are so full of anger.

Anger is simmering on that island.

I'm angry that Arnaq's anger makes me angry.

I'm angry that Arnaq's anger has ruined our friendship.

I'm angry at Arnaq's anger.

I'm angry at Arnaq.

This is the island where the crazy live.

I'm frustrated at Fia's ignorance.

I'm frustrated at Fia's decision.

I'm frustrated at Fia's sexual orientation.

I'm frustrated that Fia isn't angry.

Anger is mounting on that island.

It makes me crazy that I'm from Greenland.

It makes me crazy that I look like a Greenlander.

It makes me crazy that I'm not a Dane.

It makes me crazy that I'm a Greenlander.

The island of anger.

Angry people make me angry. The simmering anger makes me angry.

The mounting anger makes me angry.

Anger makes me angry.

I'm angry at my anger.
    I'm angry at myself.
    I don't want to be angry any more.
    Not angry

Dear Arnaq

I forgive you. I don't hate you. Move on with your life.
Take care.
Inuk

10 July

Actually, I want to see my friends. Actually, I would like to be with my family. Actually, I would like to go home to my big sister. But I can't go home because I've already escaped. I can never go back to my country. And I'm heartbroken; I've set a trap for myself. I'm terribly homesick but don't know what sort of home I'm longing for. Where am I? I'm not at home. Where am I heading? I don't have a home to go home to. Where's home to me? I don't have a home.

Today is the day. The day when I can't take it any more. The day where I've lost. Life has caught up with me. Life has beaten me. Today is the day. The day when I reach the end of the road. The day of my death. The day when I come home. Life has killed me.

Dead

My dearest Fia

Do you remember when I frightened you from inside the cupboard as you walked in? Do you remember when you locked me in the cupboard and said that it was my own fault? I remember that you felt guilty when I began to cry. I remember that you were upset because I was upset. You said: it's your *own* fault! You were right. It *was* my own fault. But because you blamed yourself, I blamed *you* because you were the stronger one. When you said sorry, I didn't say sorry. Don't get me wrong: it was my own fault that I was locked in the cupboard. It was my own decision to frighten you. I've always blamed you when I've done something bad, and that's because you're older than me. I've always blamed you for my own mistakes, and that's because you're stronger than me. My dear sister: I'm so sorry. I've become an adult. I understand now that the Greenlanders are not to blame because I escaped from Greenland. I understand now that Arnaq isn't responsible for my sorrow. I understand now that you, my dear sister, are not to blame for my mistakes. I understand now that I'm responsible for myself. Please listen to what I have to say about my last letter:

I'm grateful that you're living a happy life now. Ever since you met Peter, I've known that your relationship would end at some point because I could see that you were unhappy. I ignored your sorrow because I was afraid of having the truth confirmed. I knew that it would be a challenge when you came out and I didn't have the strength to help you through your difficult time, although I've known you were gay since we were children. I know you so well that I know everything about you. But my weakness holds me back. You've always been the stronger one, and I've allowed myself to be weak because I've always had someone to take care of me. I deeply regret this now. For the first time in our lives, it was about you, and the focus landed on me. For the first time in our lives, you were weak, and I didn't support you. When for the first time in your life you wanted somebody to take care of you, I let you go. I was weak when I was supposed to be strong. I'm sorry.

I'm glad that you've met a strong woman who you love. I'm glad that you have support. I'm glad that you don't have to be strong on your own all the time. I'm glad that you're being taken care of. I'm glad that you've found yourself. I'm grateful that you're you.

You've always taken care of me but now you must let me be myself.

You've always taken care of me but you're no longer responsible.

You've always prioritised me but now you must let me go.

You've always loved me but now you must respect me.

I feel your love.

I miss you so much that I want to fly back to be with you.

I need you so very much that I'm dying to open up to you.

But since my need for you is so great, I have to leave you.

Because I love you so much, I have to let go of you.

Forgive me.

I love you.

Your beloved, your affectionate, your brother

Late July

I feel that it's time.

As it's time, the sun is setting.

As it's time, I discover that my life, *inuuneq*, is about to end.

As it's time, I discover that my life, *inuuneq*, my human self, has disappeared.

But when it's time, *inuk*, man, emerges.

inuk says:

Find a home for yourself if you're homesick.

Don't give up when you can't find your way.

Look in the mirror if you're about to give up.

Find yourself as you look in the mirror.

You'll find your home when you find yourself: go in.

The sun will rise tomorrow.

Life begins once more.

The human being, *inuk*, will be born again, will live again.

Live your life, *inuk*. Live your life! *Inuugit!*

When it was time, my own self, my *inuk*, appeared.

When it was time, my life, *inuunera*, appeared.

When it was time, Inuk, I, came home.

Home is in me. Home is me. I am: home.

Dear Fia

I'm into men.
   Inuk

Dear Inuk

I know. You're not alone. You'll never be alone.
   Fia

The last day

Finally, I am home.
    Homo. Sapiens. Inuk.

ARNAQ

Oh, my head. I let out a deep sigh and smell alcohol. My stomach roils and I heave my body out of bed, go to the bathroom. Shit, my head is about to explode. I still feel drunk. My eyes won't focus and my legs aren't working right. I kick the clothes I dumped on the floor because they block my way and I walk five long metres to the bathroom, my hand over my mouth. My lungs are burning as I cough stale cigarette smoke out, I can no longer contain myself. Urgh! I open the toilet seat and kneel in front of it, hoping that it won't last long. My body rebels against the poison it has consumed and my stomach muscles tense so that I spew everything out. Carlsberg beer, Classic beer, vodka, tequila, Hot'n'Sweet liqueur, Arnbitter, Jack Daniel's ... It all moves so quickly from my stomach to my throat. A rainbow sprays the chalk-white porcelain like when somebody is shot in the head in a film and the wall behind him is splattered with blood. Maybe it would be more accurate to say that I puked like the girl in *The Exorcist*. It's not green but it is violent. So violent that they would have smelled it on the other side of the world if I had been standing up. It would have fallen like flat raindrops. Finally, when I'm able to take in some air again, I try to concentrate on my breathing. Through my nose, mouth and maybe ears, I vomit up hell itself, dragging out Pontius Pilate and all my intestines with it. Tears are pouring down my cheeks and my teeth are chattering. Feeling fucking awful, I think I've survived the worst. I blow the stomach acid out of my nostrils and flush the toilet. I stagger into the kitchen and rinse my mouth and my face with cold water, grab a Coke from the fridge and chug till it's half empty. My throat burns and my head is aching. It's not until this moment that I realise I need to pee and go back to the stinking bathroom. I open the toilet and see that there's still vomit on the seat and in the bowl. I spray it with cleaner, mop it up with toilet paper and flush once more. I pee and smell alcohol in my urine. When I'm finished, I turn towards the mirror and see a horrible sight. My chapped lips are the colour of red wine. My hair is still partying. My makeup is smeared all over my face and I have huge bags under my eyes. My body is trying so hard to stay alive that I can't concentrate on my polluted mind. I drink what's left of the Coke, lie down on the bed once more and take out my mobile to check the time. It's 16.07. Fuck. I think about yesterday ...

Oh yeah, baby! Friday. My absolute favourite day of the week! Oh, invincibility! Oh, bliss! Even though the town is full of people, I go to the co-op to pick up some things. Slowly, I drift into the liquor section. I always do this because I might bump into someone who will invite me to their place for drinks – and here comes the first one now. 'Hi, Arnaq!' says a voice I don't know.

'Hiii!'

I pretend that I recognise the man. Now which party did I see him at? I wonder whether I've screwed him ...

'Are you going to a party too?' he asks, eagerly.

'Yes, with Inuk and Fia. Where's your party?'

The faster I get to the point, the better chance I stand.

'It's at my place. You're welcome to come!'

'Text me, and we'll see,' I reply. I think I must have kissed him but I still can't remember his name. Option no. 1. But I think I can do better. Although I'm not going to buy food, I wander into the fruit and vegetable aisle, watching for option no. 2 to pop up. And there he is! Now this is a face I recognise. I remember this guy as somebody who's always happy to get the drinks in. He's heading towards the liquor section as I exit the aisle.

'Hey, Arnaq!' I hear him say.

'Hiii!'

I pretend I've only just noticed him.

'Ready to party?' he asks.

'Yeah, looking for a place where me, Inuk and Fia can party,' I say in a flirty voice. 'What about you?'

'We'll be partying at my house. You should come!'

'I got a new phone, and I don't have your number any more. Can you text it to me?'

I lie so that I can get hold of his name, which I can't remember. I give him a cheeky look to be sure that he'll do it.

'I'll text you. Please come!' he says with a smile. Option no. 2 is confirmed. It's a trick, you know, and it works every freakin' time! I buy booze and catch the bus just before it leaves. Today is my day.

'What have you bought?' Fia asks as I walk in.

'A bottle of vodka and some mixers,' I say.

'A whole bottle? That'll kill us!'

'What did you get?' I ask hastily.

'Four beers,' she replies.

'Four beers? I'll teach you how to party!'

I don't really want to party with somebody who has no idea how to have a good time but since she's my best friend's sister, I have to. I'll just go along and make the best of it.

'I found a party for us,' I say.

'I thought the three of us were just going to chill,' she replies, sounding disappointed.

'You need to meet some new people – it'll be fun! Their parties are good!'

'Whose parties?' She's coming round to the idea. I can't remember option no. 2's name and grab my mobile to check my texts.

We'll start in Kujallerpaat Street at nine. See you there! Enevold.

A man by the name of Enevold has texted me. I'm no longer surprised that I couldn't remember his name. Enevold. What the fuck?

'The party's at Enevold's place!' I answer hastily.

'Enevold? Who's Enevold?' she asks with a laugh.

'Enevold! What kind of name is that?' I say, laughing along with her. 'The name doesn't mean anything!' The name is not important, what's important is that he's got plenty of booze.

'Maybe his grandparents named him, poor guy,' she trails off.

'Now let's get ready!'

I turn up the volume, take off my shirt and throw it to Fia. She seems surprised to see me in my bra. Maybe she's a bit of a homophobe. I slap her ass on my way to the bathroom and laugh inside. In the shower I shave where I need to, including my pussy, and exfoliate my skin, making it nice and soft. Afterwards, I pluck my eyebrows, apply too much eyeliner, mascara a couple of times, blusher, perfume, brush my teeth, and do my hair. This afternoon, I bought a black dress that makes my ass look great, and I put it on. Oh, yeah!

'What do you think of it?'

I touch my bum and ask Fia.

'It suits you,' is all she says.

'Is that all you can say? Really?'

I jiggle my junk and dare her to say something.

'It suits you! Your ass looks good in it!'

She slaps my behind with a towel. Shyly. She looks like she's just gone beyond the bounds of propriety and it makes me laugh. She needs to get laid.

'Call a taxi, let's go to Eno's place!' I say.

'Enevold,' she says quietly.

We pick up Inuk on the way to Kujallerpaat Street.

'Inuk, my boy!'

I kiss him on the cheek as he gets in the taxi.

'Arnaq, my girl!' he replies as he gives his sister, who is in the front seat, a hug from behind.

'You smell nice; it smells great in here!' he says.

'Thanks,' I say, smiling. Inuk, my boy. My soul is happy with my dear friend by my side. My life looks brighter.

'Where're we off to?' he asks.

'E-NE-VOLD,' Fia says.

'Enevold?' Inuk says, confused.

'Eno's place. It'll be fun!' I reply.

In the entrance to the building, I feel disappointed because I can't hear anything at all. I thought the party had already started. When Eno opens the door to the flat, I see that we're early. There are some faces I recognise but they're pretty quiet. We say hello to them, open a few beers and sit scattered around the table. *How are things at school? Do you still play handball? When will the Greenlandic championships be held? Are you still seeing Lars? Oh, by the way, they've got bargains at the shopping centre. Did you see the man who went crazy at the co-op today?* Blah, blah, blah. I wait for the booze to take effect. The music is low. People are on Facebook. They're waiting for things to happen. They're waiting for the booze to kick some excitement into their boring lives. I wait.

I must have fallen asleep again and am woken by the urgent need to puke. I'm so surprised that it's already in my mouth that I accidentally swallow it again. It hurts so much that my eyes tear up and I seize the opportunity to cry a bit because of my hangover. Then I remember my handbag. My handbag! I immediately stop crying and begin to panic, searching the floor. I find it in a corner, find my wallet, hold it to my heart and thank providence. I'm safe; I haven't lost what's most important.

I can no longer stand my smell, take out my toothbrush, sit on the floor of the shower as I brush so that the water can

rinse my sticky body. I imagine that the bacteria will slide
off. The bacteria from the door handle of the pub will slide
off my hands. The bacteria from the toilet seats of the pub,
which is on my thighs, is sucked down the drain. The bacteria from yesterday's piss, which has dried on me, is washed
away. What happened last night? My brain is half dead. But
I have a feeling. I can't put my finger on it, but I have a suspicion. It will have to wait till my head clears. It will appear
as it always does. I only hope that it's not too dreadful.

'Silence is a true friend, who never betrays' – fuck that! This
fucking silence drives me crazy. I drink my Classic beer and,
irritated, I make the first move.

'Come on – blackjack?' I say loudly, picking up the cards.
They probably all feel grateful to me for rescuing them and
get into the game. I play against them all, one at a time, and
drink more than they order me to when I lose. The music
has been turned up. They're starting to sing along. They're
also starting to dance in their chairs. They laugh more.
Their faces turn kind. They look into one another's eyes. At
last, they are beginning to let go of inhibitions, and for my
part I'm changing into an animal again. I breathe in. My
body becomes lighter. Oh, the wonders of alcohol! *How are
things? It's a long time since . . . We really ought to hang out
more often. I'll let you know when I'm no longer quite so busy.*
Same old questions, but it works, you know. It works. Fia
and Inuk are no longer just talking to each other but also
turn around and speak to other people. Everyone's talking
at the same time, laughing out loud. Crates are emptied

faster and faster but I'm not worried as there's still plenty left. I'm just happy that I'm partying with people who need to get drunk, just like me. I feel the booze coursing through my veins, making me feel warm. We only have one life. I'm only human, which is why I need to let go sometimes. Tomorrow will be okay.

'Does anyone play the guitar?' somebody asks.

I feel like playing but since I haven't had enough to drink yet, I encourage others instead. The guy next to me picks it up and the others begin to sing quietly. Decency still seems to prevail over the wonders of alcohol. Shy laughter spreads. Awkwardness. I curl my toes. So awkward. I can't just sit here listening to this, so I stand over the cooker and light a cig. The song finally comes to an end, and they put the guitar back in its proper place and turn the music up loud. Because we're too sensible. Still. For a little while longer. Fia comes over to me and wants a drag. 'Enevold,' she says with a smile.

'Enevold,' I say, with a slight laugh. 'Do you think he's hot?'

'Honestly? He's sooo ugly! Have you seen his blackheads? They could pop at any moment,' she says with horror.

'But he has a prick,' I say, giggling.

'Bitch, if you're so fucking horny, you ought to find one for yourself and not for me.'

'You need to get laid, and you know it,' I say, stubbing out my cig.

'Enevold? Over my dead body! He's all yours!'

'No thank you.'

I laugh at her and go back to the table. I feel the effect of

the alcohol as I walk. I'm uplifted and suddenly I miss Inuk
so I perch on his lap. Inuk, my friend. Fia sits down across
from us, looking protectively at us, watching her younger
brother closely. I love to provoke her and stare until she
looks away. Occasionally, I tease her and wink at her. Feel
victorious when, mildly disgusted, she no longer knows
what to do. Oh, I feel invincible. And the booze makes me
come alive!

From the open window, I hear children playing, dogs bark-
ing and cars driving past. The afternoon is drawing to a
close. The sun, which hardly ever sets, is warm. Spring has
come alive, but I don't think I will survive if I go outside. My
soul is ashamed. My body has no more energy. Because I'm
just waiting for the evil to appear. Speak of the devil: I'm in
the middle of eating crisps as I feel the evil striking at my
large intestine and I prepare myself for the worst. I make
an effort and get the first evil one out. Burning and glow-
ing, Lucifer emerges as a gas from far inside my guts. As he
spreads out into the air, I almost die. Fuck. Lucifer is trying
to suffocate me. But I don't want to give in and although
I can taste him on my tongue, I run gasping over to the
window to save myself. If I had been standing up, I would
have blasted through the ceiling and got stuck in God's
asshole. That sure was a close call. I breathe in unpolluted
air by the window. I'll probably feel better once I take a shit.
I see my cash card on the window-sill and am frightened
to death. How much did I spend, I wonder? Full of dread,
I log on to my mobile banking. It says kr. 37.50 left in my

account. Oh hell! Black crack, inflammation, clotted blood, et cetera. The thought of borrowing money again makes me nervous and I'm already flooded with regrets. Regret no. 1! Fuck me! Oh, fuck the shit out of me!

The faces are nameless but pleasant enough. Enevold looks at me. Tries to sit next to me. Wants to get with me. He's trying it on so hard that I avoid looking at him as much as I can. But since I need his beers, I look at him every now and then, adding fuel to his desperation. A better-looking guy checks me out and it makes me horny. He seems to want me, which makes me feel good inside. He's option no. 1. But I don't respond – I want to see what my options are. I'm checking out women today. The need to fuck women is greater. To be on the safe side, I come up with a plan B and text Inaluk because she's always up for it. Before long we decide to go into town. To save a bit of money, I grab two of Eno's beers. On the way out of the door, I take yet another beer as one bottle is already half empty. Of course Eno pays for the taxi. Score! Before we get out, I hide the two unopened bottles of beer in my hood. There are more people than I'd anticipated and I feel really good. Oh baby, plan B is right around the corner – I can feel it! The bouncers at Hotel Godthåb recognise me and don't bother to check in my hood. Before we pass the cloakroom, I move the beers from my hood and into my handbag. Another trick. We squeeze our way through the crowd and take possession of a table. While the others make a beeline for the drinks, I open one of my beers by knocking the bottle top against the table. Oh, such a pro. The bar plays music from my childhood, which I can't deal with so I take Fia's hand and drag her out to Manhattan, the nightclub just around the corner. Lights flash, smoke is pumping out of one of the corners of the room, and the dance floor is crowded with bodies. Young bodies. Oh, that's more like it. Fia is reluctant. Just looking. No touching. But I want to move closer to the bodies. I drag her along even though she doesn't really want to come. We're now among all the bodies and I get quite close to Fia and dance for her so she can loosen up a bit. The bass is so powerful that I can feel my heart tremble. I take a furtive swig of my beer and touch Fia's body. I'm loosening her up. Doing her a favour. She's begun to touch me a bit. She dances more. Sometimes she closes her eyes. Option no. 2: I get everything I'm pointing at. And I'm pointing at Fia. You know what they say: straight until not. Straight until hot. I turn around and dance with my ass against her. We're now at one with the bodies. We want the bodies. Eyes look at us. The bodies want us. I'm feeling sexy. Fia takes my hand and leads me to the bar. I'm reeling her in.

'Four shots of vodka!' she shouts to the bartender through a crowd of people.

'Four?' I ask because I can see I'm going to pull her.

'It's on me!'

Oh, the wonders of alcohol, I tell you.

Behind Fia, *the one and only* option of all options appears. My heart begins to beat hard. I can feel the booze and my pulse is rising. Oh, ask and I shall receive!

'Fia! Did I tell you I was crazy about a woman? Do you remember that?'

She nods.

'Don't look now! There's a woman with short hair right behind you. It's *her*!'

I'm grateful that Fia isn't into women. I don't want Fia to take her away from me.

'Wouldn't it just be the same as being with a man?' she asks.

'Oh fuck, but she's so sweet! I'd marry her if she didn't have a girlfriend.'

I can get her even if she has a girlfriend. I can. I'm invincible.

'Has she got a girlfriend?' Fia asks.

'Ugh, yes. She here. She's coming over,' I say, disappointed.

Frustration rises and I feel the urge to knock her fucking girlfriend on the head and then throw her on the floor. When the bitch could no longer move, I'd take Ivik, holy fuck, Ivinnguaq, home with me!

Her girlfriend, what's-her-name, stops in front of us. I'm surprised. Does she know I've been texting Ivik? I bet she's coming to confront me. But she turns towards Fia. I watch them. Hold on . . . Fia? Fia? WHAT? Their movements make me suspicious. I look closely at them and the way their eyes meet and my suspicion is confirmed. Oh my God.

'Fia, did you hook up with Sara?' I ask, surprised, covering my mouth with my hand.

If Sara is interested in Fia, I can steal her girlfriend while she looks the other way. I can have Ivik. But Ivik and Sara have walked away, and I have a tremendous urge to get drunk. I'm going crazy because I can't have her right now. Perhaps I'll have to make do with plan B.

'No, we haven't been together ...'

'Since when have you been attracted to women? Wh–what's going on?' I ask. Straight until not, I tell you.

'How about we get out of here?' she asks.

I was beginning to feel worthless but Fia rescues me. Oh, fuck me. I'd fuck me, too.

I'm irresistible. So fucking irresistible. I go along with it after playing hard to get for a while. I'll give you a night to remember, I think to myself.

Annoyed with myself, I switch off my mobile banking and open my texts. Bring it on.

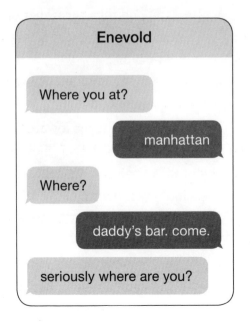

A sound from the living room surprises me and I put down my mobile. For a second I think I'm being haunted, then I remember that Fia is staying here. F. Fia. Fuck. I remember. Oh. Oh, no. Regret no. 2. Fortunately, I'm getting good at this and put it behind me immediately. It's okay. I've done worse. Compared to some of my past misdemeanours, hopping into bed with Fia is nothing. I walk into the living room half naked. Oh, I'm an expert at entrances.

'Arnaq . . .'

'Hi.' I wink at her.

'Arnaq, let's never mention this again,' she says.

Hot until cold, I get it.

'Is this the first time you've been with a woman?' I ask with some pride in my voice.

'This doesn't mean anything. Nothing happened,' she replies without looking at me.

Being snubbed is new to me. I can see that her thoughts are elsewhere so I grab some food and walk silently back to my room. I don't give a fuck. She's crap in bed anyway. Why should I care? I check my mobile again . . .

*

Oh, Fia! If I'm really being honest, she's so damn good in bed that I begin to wonder if that really was her first time with a woman. Oh, the night's going so well that I've already had a naked body next to me and it's only quarter past four. I am that good! But I can't go to bed this early. It would be like throwing the weekend out of the window. I'll sleep when I die! Inuk asks me to come out with him so I freshen up a bit and leave. The weekend has only just begun.

'Inuk, my boy!' I shout as I walk in.

He walks over to me and gives me a hug; I see the table full of booze bottles and I feel revived.

'Where's Fia?' he asks.

'She went to bed as soon as we got back. I just couldn't drop off to sleep,' I say.

I'm keeping quiet.

'I'm not surprised, the little angel,' he says.

I feel victorious. A fantastic feeling. Not even angels can resist me.

The place isn't crowded yet, but there's a good atmosphere. I grab a bottle of beer and follow Inuk, who has left the room to smoke in the kitchen. I have a lot to tell him.

'Inuk, it's ages since we've been together like this! It's so good to see you!'

'Yes, isn't it? I hardly ever see you now that you've left work. I miss you so much.'

'I'll never set foot in that place again.'

I feel my anger mounting and I take a drag of my cig.

'Are you looking for something new?' he says.

'Fuck having a boss. I want to set up my own newspaper,' I say in a proud tone of voice.

'How will you manage in the meantime?' he asks.

I don't like it when people question me but Inuk's concern soothes me and makes me feel happy. 'I always manage. You know that,' I say with a reassuring smile.

'Make sure you take care of yourself,' he says and smooths my hair.

'What about you?' I ask under my breath. 'Are you still seeing Miki?'

'Shush!' He checks to see if anyone's heard.

'Oh, come on, nobody's listening.'

He looks at me without saying anything and nods.

'Ooh! What's he like?' I ask, my voice getting loud with excitement.

'Shush!' he says seriously.

'Oops. Sorry. What's he like?' I whisper.

'He's okay. But please cut it out! Not here.'

I really don't understand why he wants it to be a secret. But I respect him and keep quiet. He only opens up to me and I value the fact that he values *me*.

'How are you doing? Are you still in therapy? Have you had a session lately?' he asks.

'Not recently,' I reply. 'Not sure if I want to go down this road tonight ... '

'Why not? It helped a lot, didn't it?' he says. He's concerned, which is nice.

Then suddenly it's like a flood, and I tell Inuk about the things that I can't open up about to other people. This takes away all the pressure that's been building up. It's not the first time that Inuk and I have opened up our hearts to one another. And I mean really opened up.

'I feel stronger than I used to. I still can't forgive my dad, but I can talk to my mum. Maybe you don't get this because you haven't experienced it, but imagine being a kid and being completely alone. There's no one you can turn to, and showing any kind of emotion is a risk. Everything has to be kept in. There are secrets, taboos, and you can't tell anybody. You have to keep the secrets. You're trapped. You just can't escape. Can you imagine what that's like? It's something that I can't get over ... '

Tears begin to stream down my cheeks, making it hard to continue.

'I can't forget the way he would come in at night, walk over to my bed and touch me ... '

Recalling this in my conversation with Inuk really hits me hard. I try to escape from my anxiety but I'm trapped in my own body. I find it harder to breathe. Shame grips me. Why do I do this? I hide my face with my sleeve. Why the hell do I start talking about this fucking shit when I'm drunk? I hold my breath until I can't any more. Why, for fuck's sake, why the hell do I keep on drinking? I sit up and go to the bathroom to rinse my face. I rinse myself in ice-cold water till my face is numb. I force myself to look in the mirror. There. I need to stop drinking! There! I've made up my mind. I can. THERE. It's done. I've had enough. I think of Inuk.

Inuk always listens, the sweetheart. I need to get a few things off my mind, and he understands. I'm so glad that I survived. Most people would have given up if they'd been through what I have, but I'm still standing. That's how strong I am! 'You haven't been let down and abused and you've received a lot of love. You'll never be able to understand. My mind ... My mind has become stronger! My soul has developed so much because I've been exposed to such horrific things! My soul ... '

I try to explain my feelings but stop when someone walks in through the door. I feel immense joy, get up and run towards her without stopping to think.

'Ivik!' I say and give her a hug.

She greets me with a nod. Oh, life's beautiful!

'What's going on? Come in,' I say, taking her arm and leading her towards the sofa. She's going to sit next to me.

'I was invited so I decided to drop by for a bit,' she says.

'I'm so glad you came! Did you get my text?' I ask her.

'What was it about?'

'Perhaps you can guess?' I say, touching her back. I want her.

'What?' she asks without looking.

I turn her face towards me and whisper to her.

'I've wanted you ever since the first time I saw you.'

She just smiles and I realise I'll have to make more of an effort. I'll do anything, ANYTHING to succeed.

'Inuk, come here,' I shout. 'Come and sit next to us!'

I introduce them to each other as he comes over.

'Inuk: this is the Ivinnguaq I've spoken to you about. Dear Ivinnguaq: this is my best friend, Inuk.'

They say hello, but then go quiet. I put my arm around Inuk's neck and move closer to Ivik.

'Inuk's into men. You're into women. I like both! Isn't that cool?'

I start laughing but soon realise that I'm the only one in the group who is.

'Arnaq!' Inuk says, pushing me aside. What's his problem? I ignore him and turn towards Ivik. Because I'm about to pull her. It's now or never.

'Miki Løvstrøm. You know him, right?' I say.

Ivik just stares at me.

'He's trying to get with Inuk. Isn't that wild?'

'What? Did you say Miki Løvstrøm?' an unknown face, sitting next to us, asks.

'ARNAQ!' Inuk shouts.

'What's going on?' another face asks.

'She says that Miki Løvstrøm's gay!' the first unknown face says loudly.

'Honestly! He has a wife and children!' someone else says.

'I'm serious! He's trying to get it on with Inuk! Isn't that true, Inuk?'

When Inuk doesn't answer, I turn towards him, just in time to see the back of him as he sprints out of the door. But my legs are too heavy. I can't go after him. Everything will be all right. Tomorrow, he probably won't be pissed at me.

My vision is blurred. My thoughts are all over the place. What's happening to my body? Someone is inside me. I'm naked. It's Ivik and I let it happen. I'm relieved it's a woman. When she stops, I'm not sure. Did I come?

'Did you call Inuk?' I hear her say but I don't quite get it.

'What?'

'Did you call Inuk?' she asks again but I still don't understand.

'WHAT?'

'DID YOU CALL INUK?'

Now my head is a little clearer.

'No, why?'

'Call him and apologise,' I hear her say.

'Why?'

I don't understand. She gives me a glass of water and

leaves. Everything's fury ... fl ... flur ... blurry ... Blurry. I'm drunk and dying of thirst. What's going on? Where am I? What time is it? I walk out of this strange room. I wade through a crowd of sleeping people sprawled on the floor. It's morning. The fucking evil sun shines right at me. I've partied till dawn. I need to go home.

Now, it's all coming back to me. I take a deep breath and hit the call button. Inuk doesn't answer and I try again. Maybe he's still sleeping. He doesn't answer and I try again. Everything will be all right. He's sure to answer this time. He doesn't answer and I try again. Come on. Please. He doesn't answer and I try again. No. He doesn't answer and I try again. Shit. He doesn't answer and I try again. I'm dying.

Shit! Crap! Fuck! Drinking is destroying me! My life's ruined! Fuck this life! My fucking hangover won't go away. My fucked-up life never goes away. Fuck life! The fucked thing will never go away! Fuck my dad! My fucking dad will never die!

It's not my fault. It's my upbringing. I didn't do anything bad. I didn't do anything evil. My *dad* is the evil one. I don't abuse. I'm the victim here. And what about my mother? She never protected me. She didn't care. I was neglected and abused: that's what's wrong with everything.

I don't want to drink any more. I've made up my mind. I'll manage it somehow. I'll make it out. Stop worrying. My thoughts are a torment. Sorrow overwhelms me. I regret so much that everything in me aches. I'm tortured by a terrifying loneliness.

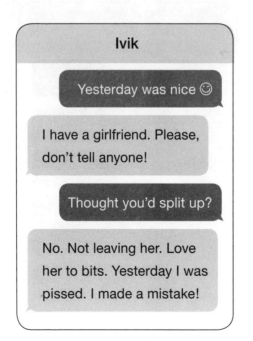

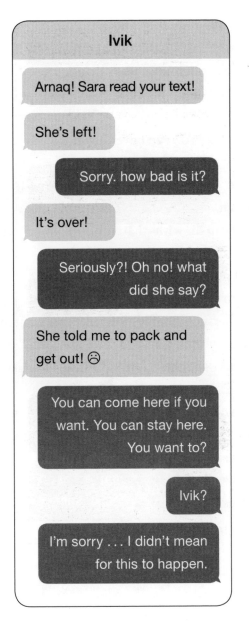

I have to conquer my fear. I have to beat it. There's nothing else I can do so I make the call and instantly feel nauseous.

'Honey?' the bitch says. She's drunk.

'Mum, I'm short of cash. Can you put some into my account?'

'My daughter! You can't even say hello?' Trying to parent me now, that's a laugh.

'Come on, help me out. I've got nothing to eat!' You're too late, bitch.

'Arnaq! Stop it with that tone of voice! Say hello to your dad.'

Oh, God no. Please, no.

'Sweetheart? My sweet daughter, my darling, my love!'

That motherfucker. His voice makes me want to throw up.

'I'm out of money. Can you send me some?'

'My sweet daughter, my darling. I miss you. Do you miss me?'

His voice changes. I recognise this voice. It's terrifying.

It's a trick, you know. I give. He gives. I give, he gives. I give, he gives. A trick.

Always has been, always will be. I give, he gives. I give, he gives.

'Yeah,' I say, almost inaudibly.

'Yeah *what*? Answer me *properly*.'

Just you wait. When I get my hooks into you one day . . .

'Yeah. I miss you.'

Just you wait. I'll stab you both.

'Do you miss me a lot?'

'Yeah, I miss you.'

Just you wait, I'll murder you.

'A lot?'

'Yeah.'

Just you wait.

'I'll put some money in your account.' That's the trick. I give, he gives. *The* trick.

I'm starving and go to the baker's first thing. Not enough money. Card declined. I pull up the hood on my coat and catch the bus. I can hardly stand up. The sun is dazzling. The motion of the bus makes me feel sick but it's still a long way to go before I'm home. Trying to stay awake. Trying to stay alive. This familiar feeling. People stare. They think: what is she doing? They think: poor thing! I think: I don't give a fuck. I decide that I just want to go home now. My body makes a sudden decision of its own accord. I get off the bus and almost run into a gaggle of schoolchildren. I need to take the quickest way home. I need to keep moving. A child is afraid of me, asking: 'Mum, what's wrong with her?' The mother says: 'Don't look! She's sick,' and gives me a dirty look. Shame. Autopilot. A teenager I run past stares at me and asks, 'What's she doing, is she right in the head?' Another mocks me, and says, 'She's a slut; just been fucked.' Embarrassment. My thoughts fall to the ground, blown away by the wind. Disappear. Nothing left. Autopilot. My brain has switched off. Autopilot is switched on. The shame stops. Autopilot takes over. All feeling dies. My body walks on.

The autopilot apparently got my body home because I'm not dead. I regret that I didn't die. You know, I give, he gives. Autopilot when I give. Autopilot when it's over. Autopilot when I've sinned. Autopilot when I'm sober. Autopilot forever.

I give, he gives.

I take another bath. Oh, holy weekend. I put on some makeup. Oh, unpredictable weekend. I fix my hair. Oh, erratic weekend. I put on some perfume. Oh, troublemaker weekend. I'm ready. Oh, delightful weekend. I'm partying again. Oh, eternal weekend. Repetitive weekend. Walking in partying circles. Ready to go again.

IVIK

I was eight years old when I first experienced it. My friend came to my classroom during playtime. She called me over. I ran happily up to her. She didn't even say hello; all she said was that she no longer wanted to be my friend and she ran off. She had covered quite a distance down the long school corridor when I began to run after her. I was always the fastest and the strongest of all the girls and I caught up with her and stopped her. 'Why are we not friends any more? Let's be friends again,' I said but she just walked away. 'You always play with cars,' she replied. 'You don't want to play with dolls.' I was upset because I liked to play with her. But I was tired of always having to play with dolls, and forgot her as soon as I got new friends. After that, I would only play with boys. Without knowing why, I discovered that I was different from the other girls.

I began to feel it when I was ten years old. One evening, we were playing football when a friend suddenly called out to me. I scored a quick goal and walked over to him. I was afraid that my team would lose and I asked him to hurry up because he was too shy to speak. 'Will you go out with me?' he asked me quietly. 'Why?' I asked, confused. 'Because you're so good at football,' he said, 'and because you're so sweet.' I said no and went back to the football pitch. I'd rather stay friends because girlfriends and boyfriends have to kiss. Lots of girls came to see us play and my friends and I began to agree among ourselves who was going to get who. They would say: 'Who are you going to ask?' 'The one with the red jacket,' I'd say. 'I was going to ask her,' one of my friends would say. 'Then the one with the glasses over there,' I'd say. We plucked up the courage and walked over to them one after the other. Some came back with a yes, others with a no. Hoping to receive a yes, I walked excitedly over to the girl with the glasses. She replied with a 'Maybe', and then after a pause, with a 'No'. 'Never mind, somebody will say yes to you,' my friends said, consoling me. Without finding it strange, I began to play football again because some people just got a yes and others just got a no. It was as simple as that. Without giving it any further thought, I began to feel that I was more like the boys. This didn't bother me at the time.

I began to question it when I was fifteen years old. We were in the after-school recreation centre, when my friend came up to me, whispering: 'I was with a girl yesterday,' he said. 'Have you been with a guy?' he asked. 'No,' I replied. 'Do you want to be with a girl?' he asked. 'I don't know,' I said. When my friends talked about getting together with girls, I felt left out. Since I hadn't dated or been with anybody, I couldn't keep up with them. Maybe I wasn't like the boys after all . . .

When I was sixteen, I began to doubt if I'd ever feel like fitting in. One day when my mum and I were alone in the house, my mum came to my room after she'd finished in the kitchen. 'Have you ever had a boyfriend?' she asked. 'No,' I

said. 'Do you think you'll have a boyfriend soon?' she per-
sisted. 'No,' I answered. All the girls I knew fell in love with
boys, which I couldn't understand. I couldn't understand
why I couldn't seem to fall in love with a boy when I was a
girl. From that point on, I began to doubt who I resembled
the most. I discovered that I was different from everybody.

I was an enigma to my friends. They didn't know which
box to put me in. When they began to question *me*, I began
to question *them*. I began to question why they called me
into question. My parents, siblings and family began to be
uncertain about me. They were uncertain about who I was.
Since my family were uncertain about me, I began to be
uncertain about myself. I was uncertain about why they
were uncertain about me.

Why do you always hang out with the boys?
  Why have you never had a boyfriend?
  Why have you never been with anybody?

As they kept asking, I began to question where I should
place myself. Since they continued to be uncertain about
me, I began to be uncertain as to who I was. I questioned
my uncertainty. They needed an answer and I felt I had to
search for it. I found an answer when I was eighteen and
moved to a bigger town to go to university. I went out one
evening with friends and a young woman I didn't know
came over to me. 'You're sweet,' she said. 'Do you have a
girlfriend?' I said no. 'But you're into women, aren't you?'

When I said no, she asked if it was all right to kiss me, and I said yes. I liked kissing this woman. After that kiss, I knew I wanted to be with a woman. I realised that I was different from everyone else. I just knew it. The answer was that I liked women.

Though I had answered my friends' and family's questions, they didn't stop asking.

'Why are you into women?'

Since I couldn't give them any reason why, I began to question the need to question it. Since I no longer felt the need to question it, I stopped questioning myself. Since I couldn't explain why I was into women, my childhood friends were no longer my friends: the ones I had fun with; the ones I got upset with; the ones I was best friends with, they all broke off contact with me because of my sexual orientation. Since I was unable to explain why I was into women, my family stopped speaking to me: my mum, who had carried me in her womb; my mum, who breastfed me; my mum, who brought me up; my mum, my own mum, couldn't forgive me. My dad, who had given me my life; my dad, who had tucked me in; my dad, who played football with me; my dad, my own dad, was unable to understand me. Since they couldn't accept that I was into women, I was no longer their daughter. They abandoned me, which was tough. It hurt an awful lot.

Now I'm twenty-three years old. My friends are my family. They don't question anything about me. They don't feel the urge. They don't ask me why I'm into women. They don't question why some people are queer. They support me. They don't desert me. I've fallen in love. I'm with somebody who doesn't have any doubts. I have a nice girlfriend, I love her and she won't leave me because I'm perfectly fine. She loves me for who I am.

I'm not asked any longer.

I'm not doubted any longer.

I'm not being abandoned any longer.

I've cleaned our apartment and the air is fresh. I've changed our bed linen and everything smells clean. I've made food and the kitchen smells good. I've lit the coloured candles. I've bought flowers for her; they're on the table. When I'm ready for her to arrive, I turn the music on and take a seat on the sofa and wait. I'm so excited about spending the evening with her. I want her to have a nice time. I want our one-year anniversary to be unforgettable.

'Hi,' she says as she walks in.

'Hi.'

I walk over to greet her and give her a kiss.

'What a nice smell; have you cooked something?'

'Come into the dining room when you're ready,' I say, smiling broadly.

She looks surprised as she walks in and gives me a hug.

'What did you make? Everything looks so nice,' she says.

'We met a year ago today. I love you.'

I kiss her. She puts her arms around me and kisses me.

'Please, sit down. Enjoy.'

I open the bottle of wine and pour her a glass. An unforgettable evening has begun. This is love. This is happiness. This is life.

'Why?' she asks.

'I don't know,' I answer.

'I'm asking you. Please answer me. WHY?'

'I don't know! I can't explain why!'

'Try. Please explain.'

'I just told you that I don't know why!'

She gets out of bed.

'Don't go!' I plead.

'Then try to explain,' she says, irritated.

'I can't explain it!' I start to cry.

She covers her naked body with a long T-shirt.

She sits next to me and strokes my hair.

'I'm not angry. I just want to know why,' she says.

'I don't know why I'm the way I am.'

'Don't you like me?' she asks.

'I like you a lot.'

'Are you bored with me?'

'No.'

'What's the reason then?'

'I've just told you, I don't know why!' I say angrily.

'IVINNGUAQ! Why won't you let me touch you?'

'Sara! Stop it!'

'WHY AM I NOT ALLOWED TO FUCK YOU?' she shouts.

I cry even harder. I don't know how to tell her it just doesn't feel right any more. She gets up, takes her duvet and pillow, leaves the bedroom and makes a beeline for the living room. An unforgettable evening. The beginning of the new question mark. The night of doubt.

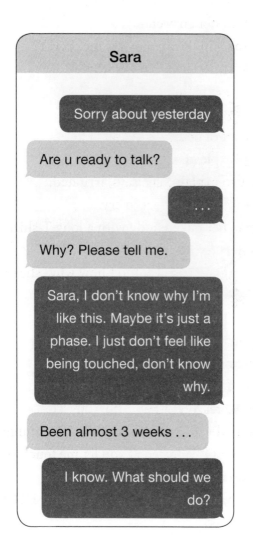

When she comes home, I walk quietly over to her. I look at her apologetically and when she gives me a little smile, I see that I'm forgiven. I hug her straight away. I love her so much that when I hurt her, I hurt myself too. For the rest of the evening, I just want to make everything good again.

'Sorry.'

I kiss her on the neck.

'Everything's fine,' she says and gives me a hug. 'I hope you'll feel better.'

'I'm sure I will.'

We hold each other close that evening. Although we don't say much, we connect. Sara doesn't try to have sex with me. I'm glad she doesn't try. Question mark. Doubt.

Today is a new day. She's on her way home and I take off my clothes. Although I took a bath this morning, I decide to take a quick shower. I wash myself thoroughly where I sweat the most. I rinse my crotch. I want to please her. I need to prove that I want her. I have to show her that I can. My short hair dries quickly. Naked, I light candles and play some music. I lie down on the bed and put grapes on my body. In my navel. Next to my crotch. Between my small breasts. On my throat. While I wait, I eat the one that's in my mouth and pick a new one. I would laugh if I saw myself. I switch off my thoughts so I won't be embarrassed. I try to think only of Sara because if I begin to think of myself, I want to get up. But I need to make an effort. I get a text and take my mobile out in small movements.

THANK GOD! My plan has been scuppered and I sit up quickly and eat the grapes. I put on my bathrobe and throw the keys down to her. At least I made an effort!

'*Iggu!* Have you been waiting long?'

'I've only just arrived,' she says and kisses me. 'Were you sleeping?'

'No, I just took a bath.'

I quickly come up with an excuse because I'm not wearing much. She takes off her jacket and opens my bathrobe.

'Knock knock,' she says.

'Who's there?'

'Ivana,' she says, letting my bathrobe fall.

'Ivana who?'

My stomach tickles.

'Ivana fuck you.'

She looks at my naked body and begins to kiss me. I take off her clothes and throw her on the bed. I switch off my thoughts and try to focus only on my want for her. I feel turned on as I lie on top of her. But then she grabs my shoulders and turns me onto my back. Silently, I turn over and get on top of her again. I start touching her. But she doesn't give up. I see her hands come closer and I panic. I try to keep still, concentrate on sensation and not what it means. But my body can't cope with it, and I jerk away. I take my fingers out of her. Before her hand gets too close, I back away; I see that she is hurt, and I immediately recoil from her. She becomes embarrassed and lies still and I have no idea what to do.

'Sara . . .'

'Why?' she whispers.

'I don't know,' I answer.

'IVINNGUAQ! WHY?' she shouts, which surprises me.

'I DON'T KNOW!' I shout back, hiding my face.

'Do you like women at all?' she asks, angrily.

'Why would you ask me that!'

'What have I done?' she says as she gets up. 'Am I doing something wrong?'

'NO!'

'Why can't I touch you? There has to be a reason why!'

I remain silent because I have no answer. I don't know.

'Do you find me repulsive?' she asks.

'No, of course not!'

'Why then? IVINNGUAQ. WHY?' Her face turns red.

'I just don't like to be touched!'

I'm frightened when she puts on her clothes. Now, I think, now she'll leave me.

'Sara, are you leaving?'

'No, I want *you* to go spend the night with somebody else! I'm not allowed to fuck you!'

'You want *me* to leave?'

I can hardly believe what she's saying.

'Yes. I want to be alone.'

'But I don't want to be alone,' I say. 'I don't want either of us to leave.'

'Well, then: explain!' she says. 'I can't carry on without an answer.'

'WHY MUST EVERYTHING HAVE AN ANSWER?' I shout at her.

She stands in front of me.

'Come back when you have an answer,' she says, handing me my clothes.

I can't stand hurting her and so I put my clothes on. I'm afraid she'll leave me if I hurt her any more and so I leave for now. I can't take being abandoned again.

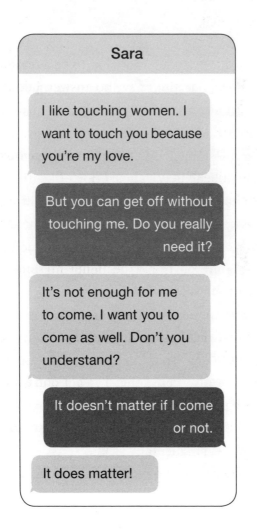

More questions, questions I can't answer, and I feel beaten. I'm being abandoned when I can't give an answer, and I'm scared. I'm afraid that Sara is going to leave me. I can't answer her questions. I don't *know* the answer. Why don't I want to be touched? Why is it I don't like it? Those fucking questions will never end and I'm tired of looking for answers. Why questions? Why answers? Why, why? People are asking questions and I'm beginning to question myself again. People are beginning to doubt me again, and I'm doubting myself again. I've been walking around town looking for an answer. I've found one. I have an explanation for Sara. I'll say that I have a disease, that I don't know what my disease is. I'll say that I need help. I'll promise that I'll feel better. I've discovered that I've got a disease. Yes, it's a disease. A polluting disease. A destructive disease. An incurable disease. I'm hurting somebody, and it hurts. Yeah, I have a disease. I'm mentally sick.

'Sara, will you listen to me?'

'Yeah, of course.'

'I think I have a disease.'

'What?'

'Down there . . .'

I don't know what to say next.

'An STD? How?' she asks me point blank.

'No, not like that. But I think something's wrong with me.'

'Does it hurt when I touch you?'

I don't know what to say so I nod. I've answered the questions. I'm lying but I don't care. I can't lose her.

'Why didn't you say anything? You should have just told me,' she says, putting her arms around me.

'I don't know . . .'

'Please make an appointment with your doctor, all right? Then you'll find out what's wrong.'

I nod. I feel relieved because she won't leave me.

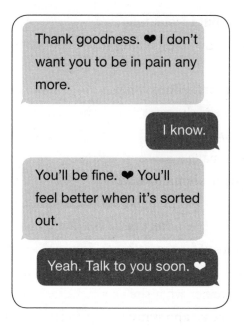

That afternoon, I go for a long walk in the mountainsides just outside the city. I'm thinking of answers. She'll say: 'What's wrong with you?' I'll reply: 'No idea.' No. I don't want her to worry about me. My reply will be that I've got a mild condition. 'What is it?' she'll say and try to Google it. My muscles are just too tense; it's something that often happens when women get stressed and it'll soon go away. I'm just stressed out. That's what they said, I'll say. Then she'll ask me, 'What will you do to make it go away?' I'll say that I need to touch myself to make myself relax because I think that's what you're supposed to do. No. I don't want to touch myself. I don't want to be touched. If I don't have sex for a longish period of time, the problem will simply disappear. This is what I'll say. I have an explanation. She'll no longer question it. She'll no longer be in doubt. But I won't find an answer to my own question and doubt. Who cares as long as I'm not being abandoned.

*

'It's been a month since you went to the doctor's, and nothing's happened,' she says.

I don't say anything.

'Will you make a new appointment?'

'Actually, it seems to have got better over the past few days,' I say.

'Really?'

Her beautiful face radiates joy. If I don't want this person, whom I love the most, to abandon me, I'll have to accept it. I have to give her what she wants. I'll have to accept being touched. I must ignore my wretchedness. I decide to do it on Friday. On Friday I'll say that it no longer hurts. But the weekdays, which normally go by so slowly, are over before I know it, and I'm not really prepared. However, I don't want to risk the terrible consequences if I put her off again. I can't imagine not having Sara by my side.

On Friday, the anxiety hits me hard. I remember that alcohol has a numbing effect so I buy two bottles of wine. I hope the drink will stifle my emotions. I only want to look at her: at what I touch. I just need to stop feeling Sara's hands. I want to be prepared. I want to be able to tackle my disease. I don't want to ask questions. I don't want to be in any doubt. Sara is my baby.

We've polished off the two bottles of wine and as I'm preparing for the inevitable, my prayers are answered.

'Why don't we pop into town?' Sara asks.

'Are you sure?'

'Yeah, we haven't been out in forever.'

THANK GOD! My plan has been ruined and I'm enormously relieved. I get to my feet quickly and get ready to leave. In the taxi, I see the apartment shrinking in the distance. As I lose sight of it, I forget the fucking bed. I throw out my fucking tormenting thoughts. We're in town; we're among people; we no longer have a place to fuck. I hold my baby's hand with ease. I move closer to her without worrying. Kiss her uninterruptedly and endlessly.

'Wait a moment, there's somebody I want to say hello to,' Sara says.

She walks towards a person who is with Arnaq, a girl who's been flirting with me. I look at Sara's body. But when I see her eyes, what I see frightens me. Sara's eyes have changed. I sense that I'm about to be abandoned and my survival instinct takes over. I can no longer dodge my fate. Sara is horny. I put my arms around her from behind, spontaneously, and kiss her neck so that she'll turn back to me. My prize.

'Knock knock,' I say with a smile.

'Who's there?' she asks, slightly confused.

'Who would you like it to be?' I ask. 'Let's go home.'

The minute we step into our apartment, I tear off her clothes and drag her towards the bedroom. She undresses me. 'Does it really not hurt any more?' she asks. 'No,' I say. Because I want it over and done with. I touch her first. It's been such a long time that I forget all the evil for a moment or two. But the evil always pops up again. As she begins to enter me, I try to go along with it. 'Does it hurt,' she asks. 'No,' I say. It doesn't hurt my fucking pussy. But my soul is in pain. It's in distress. It's being abused. And right there I realise that I'll never conquer my disease. I resign myself to being abandoned.

'Sorry,' I say with my back towards her as she tries to fall asleep.

'It's okay,' she says, trying to sound happy. 'You'll get better.'

I can hear her pain. I feel sorry for her. Hurting someone hurts much more than being hurt yourself so I put my clothes on and go out because I can't cope any more.

'I just need a breath of fresh air.'

I go to my friend's after-party and when Arnaq tries to get with me once again, I've never been less sure of who I am. But I'm beginning to find the answer to the question, and I'm scared. I'm afraid of being abandoned again, and I promise myself that I'll forget my infidelity and never ever think of it again. I can't survive being abandoned again, so I'll lie down next to my baby and resign myself to love. Sara. If Sara is by my side, then I'm happy.

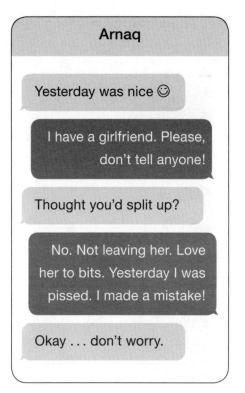

Sara

I love you ❤ What time will you be off?

Samesies. ❤ Soon.

Iggu. Will you go straight home from work or . . . ?

Yes. Anything u need?

Cool ❤ Nope, I'm good. I'll prepare something for when you get home. ☺

Nice. See you soon.

Love u love u love u ❤ See u soon. ☺

Me too.❤ c u

It won't be long now. The grapes are on the coffee table next to the freshly baked bread rolls. Check. The instant cocoa is in the mugs, ready for boiling water to be poured over it. Check. The candles are lit. Check. When I press play, a romantic comedy begins. Check. Delete texts. Check. I've cleaned our apartment and washed away the hangover smell so that she can come back to a cosy home. I've washed the clothes I wore yesterday and aired my jacket outdoors all day. I feel a bit sick but I'm drinking a lot of water and sucking a lozenge so that I can be sure to spoil her and make sure she's fine. I hear her by the entrance and take a deep breath. I check my mobile for texts. There are none. I'm ready for her to arrive.

'Hi,' I hear her say.

'Hiii,' I say from the kitchen.

I pour the water over the cocoa and walk into the corridor. Kiss her, take her handbag, and kiss her once more.

'Come in,' I say with a smile and walk back to the living room. But she heads towards the bathroom. I check my mobile once more and put it on silent mode just to be on the safe side. She comes into the living room, sees the table, smiles, and gives me a hug. I massage her back a bit and kiss her cheek.

'Please sit down, and I'll get things ready,' I say.

I stir the cocoa and sit down next to her on the sofa.

'Is everything okay?'

She nods. 'Thank you for cleaning up.'

'Don't mention it.'

I kiss her. She takes a sip of her cocoa and turns to me.

'You okay? Are you hung over?'

'No, I'm fine. I wasn't that drunk; I'm just a bit tired.'

'Where was the after-party?'

'In the block of flats downtown.'

'Did you have fun?'

'It was fine. But in the end I was so tired that I drank some water and walked home. Besides, I missed you so much.' I smile.

'You didn't come home until it was light. You must be exhausted.'

I don't want to talk about last night and so I change the subject. 'Sit down on the floor and I'll massage your back,' I say.

She sits on a pillow on the floor and I fetch some lotion from the bathroom. I return and see that she has taken off her T-shirt. I give her a kiss on top of her head while I massage her shoulders.

'My phone is out of credit. Need to top it up online,' she says. 'Let me use your phone.'

'I'll top it up on my laptop,' I say quickly.

'That will take ages. It's much quicker this way. It'll only take two seconds,' she says.

There's nothing I can do but hand her my mobile. I've deleted my texts. I tell myself not to worry. I hold my breath while my mobile is in Sara's hands.

'Who's Arnaq?' she asks, confused.

I know that I'm about to lose her and I question why I was fucking born. I begin to doubt my entire existence.

'Arnaq who?' I answer her question with a question to save myself.

'You've received a text from Arnaq,' she says. '"Hope I made you feel good last night", and then a winking emoji.' Sara reads the message aloud.

'W ... what? I don't know.'

Don't know what else to say. She's standing in front of me.

'What does she mean by that?' she asks.

'I ... I don't know.'

'Ivinnguaq ...' She smells a rat. 'Ivinnguaq, did you cheat on me?'

I can no longer keep it a secret. I can no longer hide.

'Ivinnguaq, have you been with someone else?' she asks again.

The only thing that enters my mind is she's going to leave me.

'H ... how could you?' she asks sadly.

'I don't know.'

'How could you be with somebody else? You won't even let me touch you.'

She laughs in disbelief. Then, as she goes silent, I know that now is the time. She will leave me. She is leaving me and I can't move my body. It's so awful that my body goes rigid. It hurts so much to hurt her that my soul has left my body. I see her leave. I've been abandoned.

Arnaq

Arnaq! Sara read your text! She's left!

Sorry. how bad is it?

It's over!

Seriously?! Oh no! What did she say?

She told me to pack and get out! 🙁

You can come here if you want. You can stay here. You want to?

Ivik?

I'm sorry ... I didn't mean for this to happen.

Sara

Ivinnguaq. I've had enough.

No, please don't leave me!

But I am! It's over.

No! Please come back!

I'm so sorry!

Pick up your phone!

Sara! Answer me!

Where are you?

Pack up and be gone by tomorrow.

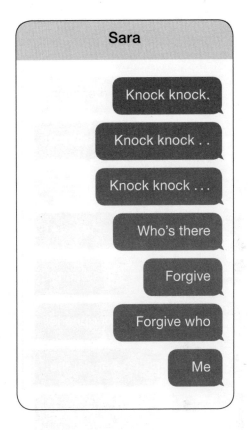

Sara

I need to talk to you.

About what?

Not about getting back together, but we still need to talk.

when?

whenever.

Now, then. Where?

Taking a stroll by the old harbour. You coming?

OK.

*

I haven't been outdoors for almost two weeks and the sunlight hurts my eyes. The dampness of spring is suffocating. The warm breeze blows in my face and the noise is painful to my ears. My soul is tortured because I torture my body. As I see her walking towards me, I can hear my heartbeat. I don't want to lose her. I feel my pain as she puts her arms around me. I really don't want to lose her. I feel the suffering I've caused her as she looks at me.

I'm losing her.

'I'm so sorry,' I say and burst into tears.

'It's okay,' she says and wraps her arms around me.

'I love you so much. I really do,' I weep.

'I know,' she says soothingly.

'Can you forgive me?'

'Ivik, look at me,' she says and lets go of me.

She holds my face in her hands and looks me straight in the eyes.

'Ivik. I'm gay.'

'I know . . . '

'Please listen to me,' she says. 'I'm into women. I'm not into men.'

I can't admit what she's trying to tell me.

'Because I like women, I can't be with a man,' she repeats.

'What do you mean by that?' I say, even though I know.

'I can't be with you.'

I stare at her.

'I can't be with you because you're a man.'

She's revealed the answer to the eternal question. The answer I haven't said.

'But I don't want to lose you,' I say and begin to weep again.

'You won't lose me. I'm by your side. I'm right here.'

'What do we do now?' I ask.

'I can't be your girlfriend,' she says.

'I know.'

'But like I said: I'm by your side. I'll have your back. I'll be your friend.'

'Please don't leave me.'

'I'll never leave you.'

The sun brightens my eyes, which have only seen the world in black for a long, long time. I can smell the previously frozen earth melting. The warm breeze sounds like a song. My soul finds solace in my body. Now that my body has finally found *the* answer, my soul is no longer in doubt.

I was born again when I was twenty-three years old. I was born as Ivik.

SARA

04.32

The spring night comes alive. The blue sky is dawning. The sun's rays hit the mountaintop of Sermitsiaq and the north-eastern sky is a bright red. The rays move slowly down the mountains, melting the frost on the ground. The night has frozen the earth but as soon as it melts, the cold will dissipate. The last snow thaws, trickling quietly down, and as soon as it disappears, the harsh temperatures of winter are forgotten. The spring night is silent. There's no wind. The sea is calm and the waves lap at the beach. The warm sun awakens the birds, who have slept through the cold night, and they begin to sing. The reappearance of spring is pure, generating calm. I walk through the empty streets. I have hardly slept and the cool air chills me. It makes me shiver and I tense my muscles. Soon the sun will warm my skin and I will forget the cold night. As spring comes alive, my body is slowly revived. The stillness gives me the energy to begin the day.

#calmbeforethestorm

I breathe in fresh air before I go into the hospital in Nuuk. I drink in the stillness before leaving it behind. The corridors are empty. But I can hear the faint sound of a voice in pain. I take a deep breath and walk in the direction it came from.

On the way, I go to the toilet and wash my hands. Once they are clean, I pull myself together and walk in the direction of the sound. I need to be strong. I open the heavy door. Her face is drawn and her body tense. You can see that she is in pain, yet her eyes say something else. The anxiety and joy on her face strike me.

'How's it going?'

'Five centimetres,' she says with a smile.

'Is that much?'

'Yeah, but I'm only halfway there.'

'What time did it start?'

'I had contractions around ten o'clock last night.'

'Why didn't you call me then?'

'I did when I knew for sure that I was about to give birth. I thought I'd let you sleep a bit longer,' she says.

'Next time, call me immediately!'

'Next time? There won't be a next time!' She groans in sudden pain.

A contraction hits and I begin awkwardly to massage her back. I'm about to be an aunt.

#pain #nowayback

06.14

As her contractions grow more intense, the bones in my fingers are nearly crushed but all I feel is what my sister is going through. Her face is dark red. Her body is so bloated that I'm sure a needle prick would make her explode. Out of the corner of my eye I see what is trying to come out and I'm shocked. I make an effort not to faint and I try not to imagine that a big head is working its way out of that tiny opening. This just isn't possible. I don't know what it looks like.

Honestly, I really don't know what it looks like.

'I'm gonna be sick! Bag!' she says urgently.

I take an open bag, hanging by the bedside, and hold it to her mouth. I'm relieved that she doesn't vomit after all. She has another contraction, and I forget the purity of the night. I stiffen because I'm confused and look to the midwife for guidance. She gazes at me in silence and I realise there's nothing I can do. An infant is about to be born and all we can do is wait. My sister can no longer control her body, which takes over. Her conscious mind disappears as she begins to push and I tighten all my muscles. 'Breathe in and out. Breathe,' the midwife says.

I realise that every time she tells my sister to do so, I've been holding my breath as well.

'I can see the head,' the midwife says.

My thoughts are buzzing so much that I can no longer keep track. I stop thinking. With my sister's hand in mine, I move closer to the baby, which is being born. She pushes once more and the head suddenly appears. I see its hair.

'If you push one final time, the baby will be out,' the midwife says.

My sister listens only to her body and no longer hears her. She already knows that her child will come out when she makes that last push. She gathers all her strength in preparation. She pushes one final time and I can no longer hear anything. When the child's shoulders appear, the rest of the body glides out. A transparent fluid follows. Blood splashes. But my eyes only go to the beautiful baby and I'm paralysed. I'm transfixed as the midwife lifts up the newborn, with its head down, and gives its tiny body a gentle thump. I realise that it has not yet cried. It is not breathing. I hold my own breath. I won't breathe out until the baby begins to breathe. Breathe, I pray. Breathe. Its small arms and legs begin to move. Its groggy face grimaces. A loud cry comes out and I exhale. My body can no longer contain the magnitude of my emotions and I feel tears trickle down my face. The child breathes. I turn to look at my sister. She is disoriented but understands that the child has been born when I smile at her. I kiss her on the forehead. I experience once more the purity of the night.

'Will you cut the umbilical cord?' the midwife says. I look at my sister for permission. Her smile answers my question. The midwife hands me a sterilised pair of scissors and I sever the child's link to its mother. I separate them. The child is now a human being. An individual. The midwife lifts the child, puts it on my sister's chest, covering it with a blanket. Although this is the first time my sister sees her baby, I can tell she feels she has always known the child. I see her tears and begin to sob myself. Nothing can surpass love.

Only several minutes after the birth, we realise that we don't know the gender of the child. We haven't given it any thought. I was too dazed when cutting the umbilical cord, and now the baby is covered with a blanket. Also, it doesn't really matter what sex the child is, I think. I can see that my sister thinks the same, but the midwife congratulates her on a baby girl.

'A little girl,' she says.

'A little girl,' I say.

A pure child.

'Would you like to hold her?' she asks.

She sees me hesitate, looks at me questioningly.

'It's not difficult. You just sit down on a chair and hold her like this,' she says.

'That's not it. My hands are dirty.'

The child's purity is immensely valuable to me. I don't want to dirty it with my hands.

'Then go and wash them,' she says, chuckling.

'No, it's okay,' I whisper.

Dirty hands shouldn't touch. A polluted soul shouldn't pollute others. A black heart shouldn't love.

#pureheartandblackheart #dontgotogether

08.26

I walk out of the hospital and forget the cold night. The sun shines bright. The town is alive. The streets, which were empty before I went inside, are now filled with people, all rushing somewhere. I stroll to the shops and greet everybody I pass. Most of them see my smile and can't help reciprocating, and I ignore those that don't. I want to be blind to all negativity. I won't see it. My stomach rumbles and I realise I'm hungry and walk to the co-op's café. Who cares that it's morning, I buy a French hotdog. Through the plate-glass windows, I gaze at people who are just waking up from their night's sleep. There is too much ketchup in my hotdog and I get some of it on my fingers but I don't care. Today I can eat anything. I squeeze out some of the excess ketchup onto my plate and take a gulp of the coffee. It tastes watery and I doubt it's even coffee, but I don't give a fuck. Today, I can drink anything. I've finished eating, but I sit and watch the people walking past. Off and on, I find myself daydreaming and hope that the woman I'm thinking of will suddenly appear in the crowd. But I know this won't happen, so I don't let myself hope for too long, but it's okay. Today, I can accept it. I buy something to drink and decide to go home and rest my tired body. I get into a taxi with a driver I've never seen before. Taxi drivers are all different. Some don't speak; some break the ice by talking about the weather; others tell a little story. But my taxi driver today seems like a real chatterbox.

'Isn't it a gorgeous day?' he says for a start.

I could have chosen not to answer but decide to give him the chance to talk. I'm pretty sure that he'll talk non-stop all the way but I don't give a fuck. Today, I don't mind listening. And so he begins chatting away, telling me his story . . . and it goes like this . . .

'I'm really looking forward to getting off work. Work is tough when you know you'll be slammed. I think there's something going around because I feel like I'm catching a cold. I never have trouble getting up in the mornings but this morning I really did, and guess what? Now I've got a headache. It's incredible. I nearly decided to stay at home but my work is very important to me so I took a painkiller instead. You see: I don't know what to do with myself when I'm not at work. I was at sea for ten years, from my teens, and I was hardly ever ashore. I began to work as a fireman after I got married, which would have been thirty years next year if I'd stayed in that job. Thirty long years. How often do you think I went on holiday in all those years? Three times! Three times in thirty years! I just don't know how to be on holiday. I'm not sorry to be taking more time off now. You see, my mum's getting old and I spend my free time with her. I'll be okay when she passes away because I've lost so many people since I was a child that I'm used to it. That's life, isn't it . . . She's a bit senile, which is kind of funny. You see, when you get older, you start to forget things.

'My ex is having me over for dinner this evening because our daughter is in Nuuk so we'll all eat together. And I almost forgot. My daughter went to boarding school in Denmark from the ages of fourteen to seventeen and now she has a job and hardly ever comes to town. But I've learned how to Skype so I still sometimes see her that way. I'm not really into these modern gadgets because we grew up in hard times and had to make do with very little. It was a simple time. So I'm not bothered about all these modern devices. My daughter is the opposite: she always wants something new, but that's okay. If she's broke, I always give her money. You see: I'm so generous that it gets a bit silly sometimes . . . Here we are, that'll be 97 kroner.'

The taxi driver has told me his entire life story for only 97 kroner, but from his story I gather what really happened:

he got drunk last night and had a hangover this morning. He was about to call in sick but then remembered all his unpaid bills and went to work anyway. He quit working at sea and went ashore because he couldn't keep his job. When he was no longer able to control his drinking, he was urged to quit his job as a fireman and now he earns a living driving a taxi. He has never been close to his mum but now that she doesn't have much time left, he tries to show that he's a good son. His wife left him. He gives money to his daughter in order to keep in touch with her . . . He wants to be heard. He wants to exist. He tries to avoid being lonely by talking about himself. If he had bothered to ask me, I would have told him that I just witnessed a child's first breath, but I don't give a fuck that he didn't ask. Today, I resist the temptation to criticise anybody, and decide to show patience instead.

'Thank you,' I say with a smile.

'Same to you. Have a nice day,' he answers.

I'm sure I will have a nice day. I don't give a fuck about negativity. Today a little baby was born; today must remain pure. Polluted thoughts must not ruin this day of purity. Today, my hands must not get dirtier.

#dirtyhands #thetaxidriverandi

I get home and all my muscles relax because the universe can no longer see me. That fucking false smile. I take off my smile because nobody will know, except maybe the Heavens and I don't give a fuck if they do. The invisible sense can't touch me because it's insubstantial. Now I can listen to music in peace and regain control of my unruly body. My brain has tried to be positive all day but disturbing thoughts are about to overwhelm me so I calm down with some music. 'Home' by Foo Fighters kicks in in the speaker. A black cloud hovers over me. Darkness welcomes me. Darkness brings loss with it. Forgiveness. Letting go. Just being. Feeling safe once again. Darkness brings burdensome emotions with it. Hard work. But darkness also brings its good friend with it: light. No thanks. Not ready. I change the music in the middle of the song. 'Walk of Shame' by Pink. That's more like it. Brightness welcomes me. Brightness brings celebration with it. Getting girls. Sex. Carefree life. Blame it on the alcohol – I'm innocent. The alcohol is the bad guy here. I'm not evil; it's the alcohol that causes problems. But light also brings the after-effects of the alcohol with it. Spending the next day puking. Facing the fucking consequences of my recklessness. The brightness also brings its fucking companion with it: regret, which obviously never occurs until it's too late. Regret, which is linked to dirt. Dirty hands. Today must remain pure, which is why, sadly, I'm unable to feel the light emotions; even they make you dirty. Today I am not going to be even dirtier than I already am. I don't want to be dirtier today. I want my thoughts to be pure. I change the music once again. Rihanna. 'Stay'. The real world greets me. The real world arrives every day and the real world hurts. My anger is tremendous. This brings torture with it. Torture. Questions. Fucking depression. Depression drags neglect with it. I try to drag myself, skirting reality. In vain. Guilt. Recriminations. Analysis, which

I don't have the energy for. Reality brings dying love with it. Love's companion: sorrow. I don't want to face reality. I want the day to be joyful and I have to try to avoid the truth. The purpose of today is to be unforgettable and happy, and if I let it fill up with sorrow, I risk reality dragging me down to hell, which makes me change the song once more. Joan Jett and the Blackhearts begin 'Crimson and Clover'. The world of dreams bids me welcome. Fuck. Daydreams are accompanied by forbidden emotions. The king of emotions, ungovernable ruler of emotions. Fuck. Daydreaming brings with it a face, which only appears in my thoughts. A body, which I can only feel in my body. Out of reach. Shit. Daydreaming brings suffering with it. Not being able to touch what you yearn to touch. Not being able to have what you yearn to have. Not being able to taste what you yearn to taste. Fuck! So much pain! But daydreaming also brings along its good friend: hope. Hope that can't become reality because it's nothing but a dream. Hope you can't hope for. Today, hope will not turn me into a prisoner. I walk over to switch off the music, but I don't quite manage to. Music can change mood but I'm unable to find joy in these songs. What to do. Hmm. Something else can replace joy: indifference. I turn up the bass and put on some techno. I don't even know whether it's really techno. Some shallow, meaningless and boring song, which drowns all emotions. The kind of music that's played in discos. A bit like a stupid bitch or a douchebag with a big mouth.

#happiness #idontgiveafuck

10.59

Today will be a day of joy. I begin by tidying up my room a bit and changing the sheets. Today is an unforgettable day. I dust everywhere with a cloth. Today, I must be thankful. I dust every corner and vacuum, even under the bed. Today, I must be happy. I open the windows and wash the floor. I do it all over again just to be absolutely sure that I didn't miss a bit. Today, I must smile. When I'm through, I look at my clean room. I don't feel satisfied and move to the kitchen. Because today is a good day. I do the dishes till my hands are red and irritated. When the kitchen is in order, I move on to tidy the living room and clear the hall. I vacuum, because why not. I wash the floor because I might as well. Twice. When I've finished cleaning the whole apartment, I sit down. Today is a day of joy. The apartment is clean. But my hands are still dirty. But then again, today is a (motherfucking) day of joy!

#iamahappymotherfucker

12.50

I just can't figure out how not to care. I just can't figure out how to shut things out; I can't figure out how to pretend when I feel bad. I just can't figure out how to smile when I'm angry. I just can't pretend to be happy when I'm obviously upset. My whole apartment is spotless but my hands are still dirty. My attempt at a day of joy was a flop. Of course, the birth of the baby is truly unforgettable but I can't help feeling sorry for her because of all the challenges in life that she will face. I already feel sorry for her that she'll stumble and bleed when she gets bigger. I already feel sorry for her that my sister will tell her off. I already feel sorry for her because she'll have low self-esteem when puberty hits. I feel sorry for her because one day she'll fall in love. It's a shame that she'll be abandoned one day. That one day she'll have to break up with somebody. That she'll get lost trying to piece together her broken heart. That she'll be angry. I feel sorry for her that she'll be lonely. I already feel sorry for her that she was born. My attempt at a day of joy is a failure and I give up. I just sit down and return to reality. After all, life is shit. The light doesn't shine when you're in the dark. The day is dark. The day of pity. I have no compassion for myself. I destroy all that I touch, and I'm not surprised that darkness not only captivates me but holds me captive as well.

#realitycheck

All the questions that I am unable to find an answer to surface once more, infiltrating every crevice like tiny worms. I grab my iPad and log on to Facebook. Four notifications. Congratulations that I'm now an aunt. Some likes of my photos. Games requests. Tag from my sister. I click it. She has posted a single photo. My sister is holding the purest child in her pure hands. Her weight and height. Time of birth. Many different people have commented on the photo with no congratulations, asking about the gender of the baby. Later on, my sister's added that it's a girl, which is when the same people congratulate her. I find our society fucking unbelievable. I look at the sweet little baby before I go to my news feed to see whether there's anything new or interesting. There isn't, so it's time for my regular routine. Search, click. Ivinnguaq, click. Nothing new. Is she alive, I wonder? I hope so. I click on our conversation. 'Active 45 minutes ago.' Yes. She's alive. The next person I want to check is hope without hope, so I hold back so I won't look like a stalker and get up to wash my hands. When I get back, search, click. Fia, click. Shit. She finally changed her profile picture. I'm unable to see all of her photos because we're not friends on Facebook, so I gaze at her new profile picture for quite a while. I catch myself smiling. I hover over 'Add friend' for a long time. No, if she was really interested, she would have sent a friend request. I log off. Go to Google. Google knows everything.

Search: Sooruna Ivinnguaq attortikkumaneq ajortoq?

Results: Your search did not match any documents. No wonder.

Search: Why doesn't Ivinnguaq want me to touch her?

Results on Knr.gl: 'The Government of Greenland will pursue a responsible economic policy.' Oh, politics.

Results on site from random Danish school: 'This means that if you have contracted the Influenza A virus, you will not contract it again.' Thank God?

Search: Why was Ivinnguaq unfaithful?

Results: This is why men are unfaithful – sex and partnerships: 'Is it okay to be unfaithful so long as nobody finds out? Read here when and why men's reptile brains take over and other women ...'

Hetero bullshit.

Search: Why do I feel guilty?

Results: Danish football player confesses – I feel guilty. 'Maybe this was the only mistake I made during the entire match but that didn't matter, because we lost anyway ... I feel incredibly guilty towards ...' I hear you. I know how you feel.

Search: Why do lesbians cheat?

Results: 'I'm unfaithful and don't know what to do.' Hetero bullshit again.

Scroll. 'Inspiration: How do lesbians have sex?' Fuck you. Scroll.

'Lesbians never smile.' You said it! Scroll.

I receive a text message on my mobile and I'm back in the room again.

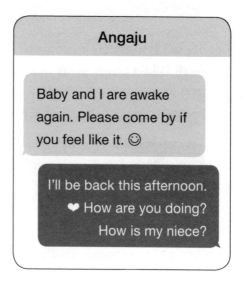

Angaju

Baby and I are awake again. Please come by if you feel like it. ☺

I'll be back this afternoon. ❤ How are you doing? How is my niece?

We're both doing great. She's the cutest ❤ So I've made up my mind on the name I mentioned – it suits her.

Really? Ivinnguaq?

Ivinnguaq ❤ Or Ivik (if she feels more like a boy) ☺ You never know. Is that OK with you?

Why wouldn't it be? It's perfect ❤ Is Ivik a boy's name?

It's typically used for boys but can also be for girls. But then mostly as Ivinnguaq, as you know ☺

OK, I'll be there in a few hours. See you ❤

#venus

13.02

Just found the very last piece that's been missing for a century. Fuck Google.

All of a sudden, I've found the answer to the riddle that has been bothering me for ages. It feels like finding the last piece of a jigsaw puzzle with 1000 pieces, which has been lost in a pocket in a pair of trousers you never wear. It feels like finally putting it in place. I realise I haven't been treated badly and I haven't treated anybody badly either. I realise why my (ex-)girlfriend, Ivinnguaq, never wanted me to touch her. I realise why she's been unfaithful to me. I realise why Ivinnguaq wanted to be called Ivik. I realise that Ivinnguaq *is* Ivik. I realise that my ex-girlfriend is a man. Although I've already put my shoes on, I walk about in my clean apartment, getting ready to leave. I have to breathe fresh air into my lungs, to get them breathing again after a long time without oxygen.

I walk towards Kolonihavnen, the old harbour, and I don't look at passers-by – or, to be more precise, I look at them but I don't see them. At the last minute I notice an acquaintance smiling at me and I return the smile when she has already passed by. It's not until after a black cat has crossed my path that I remember I'm afraid of cats. It's not until after I have crossed the road that I remember it's illegal to cross here, and a driver gives me an annoyed look. I can't see the screen on my mobile because of the sun and so I sit down on a bench in the shade. I send a text, fervently hoping that he wants to meet me because I feel such an urge to put things right.

'Yes,' he answers.

I smile at the thought of our relationship; I haven't had a *girl*friend, but a *boy*friend.

Old introduction: 'Ivinnguaq, my *girl*friend.'

New introduction: 'Ivik, my ex-love, but my new friend.'

#mars

Departure. Goodbye. There are two kinds of departure. Departure with closure and departure without closure. Ivik has closure and has said goodbye. But my exit feels half-hearted. It's necessary to forgive. But for me it's more important to be forgiven. Ivik cheated on me because he felt like a man. I forgive him for that. But I don't feel forgiven for breaking up with him. He says that he's forgiven me. He agrees that we can't be together. But I feel guilty anyway. Forgive. Be forgiven. If the first doesn't happen, the second won't work. You can't be forgiven if you haven't done it yourself first. And then saying goodbye will seem half-hearted, and if this is how it feels, saying goodbye won't be a real departure. One of the things the sweet baby will experience one day.

But maybe I can protect her. I can protect her from all evil. My love for her is so strong that it hurts. My heart aches. I can hardly handle the thought of her in kindergarten because that is where she'll learn to be bad. She'll need to be forgiven when she misbehaves. And she'll feel hurt. School is where she'll be surrounded by naughty children. She'll have some bad experiences there. And she'll get hurt. I feel an urge to fetch and kidnap her right now. I feel an urge to escape with her so that she'll never be marked by the world, but that would be something her mother would never forgive me for. Would the child forgive me, I wonder? It wouldn't matter. All that would matter would be that she's not hurt. I would be a mountain nomad with her. God, what kind of thoughts are these and where the hell do they come from? What a way to say goodbye. What a day on which to say goodbye.

#notpossible #impossible

14.34

Some people are destined to change the world. They give love. They have the power to forgive. They work hard for what they believe in. They gain the public's attention. They are the few people useful to society. These people must be supported since they are the ones that are valuable and have something to give back. Then there are all the rest that must support the few. These people must sacrifice themselves so that the good ones can be successful in life. Very stupid of me to think that I was the first kind of person. I am the second kind. One who is easily expendable, which I'll have to accept. I will sacrifice myself because I have nothing else to give. I'm not a fighter. I'm not worth fighting for. Until today, I fought to prove the opposite. But no matter how much I fight, I spoil everything I touch, and there must be a reason why. It's not just a coincidence. And it's even on a material level: I've lost count of how often I've broken other people's belongings. I've lost count of how many times I've spilled coffee on somebody's book or newspaper. I've lost count of how many times I've stained somebody's chalk-white sofa with chocolate or ice-cream. I should have taken this as a wake-up call a long time ago because then I might not have wrecked so many lives. I just thought: 'Next time I won't do it; next time things will be okay; next time things will work out.' Now, however, I realise that I don't have what it takes to be successful. After ruining not just one but several lives, I'm finally ready to give up. I'll ruin the little baby if I don't. My one objective is that the child will be a success. It's either me or her. If she's going to have a good life, I must sacrifice myself. I'm not worth fighting for. She's worth dying for.

#1 #2

I feel torn. I'm restless. It's hard for me to accept that I might never be happy again. But then again: I have to accept that my life won't revolve around me. I'm satisfied as long as the child is okay. At least I'm trying to convince myself. A pure heart mustn't love a dark heart. The child is alone but that's fine because her heart is pure. My heart is dark. Polluted. I'm a bad person because I broke up with Ivik. I'm not a bad person just for breaking up with Ivik. I'm a bad person because of the things I did while we were still together. I can't believe that I ended it because he cheated. Because I was busy cheating in my thoughts. Since I met Fia, I've been unfaithful with her in my head. If I had run into her, I would have been the one cheating first. I'm convinced that if we had been alone at some point, I would have been unable to control myself: I regret even now that I didn't kiss her when I met her for the first time. I regret that this is how I think. I didn't leave Ivik because he was unfaithful to me. I left him because I was hardly any fucking better myself. He believed that I left him because he had done something terrible. He believed that he was a bad person. Now that he's forgiven me, what puzzles me is that I can't move on myself. The fact that Ivik has moved on doesn't make me feel any better. Since I left him, I've truly wished that he'd get on with his life because it hurt so much to be hurt. I would have sacrificed anything for him to move on. But now it hurts because he finally let go of me. Maybe I like to hurt people? Maybe I feel hurt when I haven't got anybody to hurt? I'm now alone in the world. Ivik has let go of me and I no longer mean anything to anybody. Although I'm relieved that Ivik is feeling better, it hurts to know that I'm all alone now. I don't matter to anyone. But I would matter if I sacrificed myself for the child. What I want can't happen and therefore doesn't matter, but I can make her dreams and wishes come true. I can sacrifice myself for her. This is why I keep on even if I don't want to. For once, I must succeed. For once, I must be useful. For once, I have to repair what I've ruined. I have to keep trying till I die. Dead woman walking.

#dietrying

15.24

When something is born, something dies. This is something I can't deny. I walk past sick people and look around in the corridor. I catch sight of my sister who is breastfeeding her baby in one of the rooms. I stop by the door. My sister sees me and smiles and I can see that she notices I'm feeling down. Depressed.

'How is she?' I ask before she asks.

The baby is dressed in white and wears a white cap. She looks like a little angel. She *is* a little angel. When she spits out the nipple, she begins to suck her sweet lips. She's so dear that my heart almost explodes. I take a deep breath. I'll do anything, I think; it's all worth it.

'How are *you* doing?' my sister says.

I just look at her. No matter how hard I try, I can't lie to my sister. She always knows. I don't try to lie because it won't work. We often think of the same thing at the same time. My brain is hers and her brain is mine. Yet our hearts are different. When I miss her, she may call me without knowing that I miss her. I feel pain when she feels pain. She feels pain when I feel pain. I can tell that she feels my pain right now.

'Has something happened?'

'I've spoken to Ivik.'

'Ivinnguaq? What did she say?'

'Did you realise that she feels like a man?'

She nods.

'I've had a *boy*friend.'

'Actually, I think you've known it all along. At least you tried to be with a man once in your life,' she says, smiling.

'Maybe I did know, deep down. He felt better after we talked, so that's good.'

'What about you?' she asks, putting her hand on my back. I hunch my shoulders. I don't want to cry. She sees it on me and lets me compose myself.

'Now you sit down in that armchair over there. Everything will be all right when you hold the baby.'

'No, it's all right.'

'Sit down!' she smiles.

I can't keep denying her so I sit. There. I'm sacrificing my heart for the child. When my sister hands me the baby, she immediately starts to cry. I'm shocked and try to hand her back to my sister but she quickly moves out of reach.

'Don't worry. She'll stop in a minute,' she says.

I just can't cope with her crying and, panicking, I begin to console her.

'Just take it easy,' my sister says.

I relax my muscles. I cradle the baby gently as I talk to her. She stops crying and it's as if the whole world stops. She breathes quietly. Her facial muscles loosen up. I gaze at her delicate lips. She tightens her face once more and just when I think that she's about to cry again, I realise she's smiling. A very happy smile. As if somebody reassured her while she was worried. As if somebody said something lovely to her while she was upset. As if she's no longer alone after having been lonely. I look at my sister. *Did you see that?* I ask with my eyes. She nods. I feel my heart beating. I've just witnessed one of the wonders of life, and a gratitude grows inside me that I haven't felt for a long time. Things will be all right, I feel; life's okay. I forget the coldness of the night.

'Welcome,' I say to the little baby in my arms. 'Welcome.'

She's given me joy that I can't describe. I think of all the fantastic things that joy will give her, and I smile. Life has many challenges to offer, but love's small miracles will always win. I've sacrificed my dark heart and it dies. Light replaces it. I've sacrificed my dark heart and it dies. Instead, light is trickling into me. I'm whole once more. I've sacrificed the darkness in me. The darkness in me dies. I sacrifice myself; I die but am born again. When something dies, something is born.

#welcomebacktolife

18.47

I must have fallen asleep with the child in my arms and I wake up with a start. Time no longer means anything when I see her sleeping peacefully. The things going on in the world right now no longer mean anything. For the past few months, I've felt like shit from the moment I woke up, and now that feeling has disappeared. I would often wake up and immediately feel that I didn't have the energy to face the day. I would often have to force my heavy body out of bed. In fact, I'd given up finding the purpose of life. Now my body is so light that I'll almost be able to fly when I get out of bed tomorrow morning. My thoughts are so wonderful that I can't control the smile on my lips. I kiss the child and give her to my sister.

'Are you feeling better?' she asks.

I nod.

'What about the woman ... What's her name ... Fia? Have you heard from her?'

'No. She's not interested in me. But that's okay,' I answer.

My body is suffering because I can't get what I long for. I become restless whenever I think of her. I burn when I see her. My body aches for her. But there's nothing I can do about it. If she doesn't feel the same for me, it's no good hoping.

'Her loss,' my sister says, kissing my cheek.

'My loss,' I say. 'You should see how beautiful she is!'

'What are you doing here then? Find her – after all, Nuuk isn't that big.'

'Nuuk is big when there's somebody you actually want to bump into. People you don't want to see pop up all the time, but people you want to see are nowhere to be found,' I sigh.

'She's bound to show up some time.'

'Anyway, what would be the point if she did? I would just feel worse because I can't have her.'

'Then *do* something or other. Go out with your friends. You'll go crazy if you act like a hermit,' she says with a slight laugh, pointing towards the door. 'Now get out of here.'

I laugh, give her a hug and kiss the baby. I walk out as a completely different person from the one who walked in. I feel I've got a new chance to make something of my life and I want to take it. I want to start afresh. The town is quiet now. The sun is lower in the sky but it's still light. A strong feeling of joy hits me and my otherwise dead body wants to move. I run home to fetch my bike and off I go. My lungs can hardly cope with the tall hill by the airport but I can finally feel my weak muscles beginning to come alive. Without stopping, I reach the top and gasp for breath. My muscles are working, and I can feel the blood circulating around my body. My heart is beating. Still I really need to feel that I'm alive. I reach the steep road down towards Qinngorput, the newest area of Nuuk, and stop. When I was a kid, I would zoom down the tall hills just to feel the excitement. Now I want to feel alive. I want to feel the pain if I fall. I want to feel the relief if I don't. I want to *feel*. I'm calm for a moment then I begin to pedal hard. Soon I'm going really fast and the wind sings in my ears. The handlebars are hard to control. I veer off course almost without touching them. I approach a couple who are out for a walk and although I realise that they might quickly change direction, I race so close to them that my heart nearly stops. The road is turning and I cycle out into the middle of it. If a car comes, most likely I'll be badly hurt. I might die. If I'm supposed to live, no car will come. If I'm supposed to die, then a car will come. It's that simple. I turn with the road and my heart hurts. I'm so nervous that I almost stop breathing. Adrenalin kicks in hard as the possibility of death is just around the bend but I'm cycling too fast to change my mind. I hope no car will come. I reach the curve in the road and my heart is pounding. I gasp for breath. I feel saved. No car is coming. I can't help being amused at myself and laugh out loud. The road straightens out and although I'm going fast, I lift my hands from the handlebars. Tears begin to pour down my cheeks from the strong wind, and once more I head right towards the middle of the road, and I close my eyes. The heaviness in me is blown away and disappears. My body will survive. I've arisen from the dead.

#chance #change

21.56

I lie down on my small sofa and switch on the music. I can't seem to find the right songs so I listen to some instrumental music instead. I'm not ready to go to bed because all the amazing things that have happened today are bouncing around my head. I feel that Ivik's forgiveness is beginning to help. I'm human, I can't ignore my needs any more. I forgive myself for the breakup. I forgive myself for thinking of somebody else. I'm only human. But I can't stop thinking of Fia. Her beautiful face pops up among my many thoughts. My stomach fizzes every time I think of her. Every time, I smile. But I distract myself when it happens because hope is too dangerous! I reassure myself that someday I'll find the right person. I just can't imagine not having Fia. I have to accept that I'm alone. I was born alone, and I'll die alone. Being alone isn't all bad. It's enough that somebody loves you and you love somebody. If you love yourself, you're not lonely when you're alone. Look at me, all positive. I listen to the guitar in the speaker, my heart exposed. When the song ends, a new one begins. I recognise the song and shiver: it's the song I listened to when I was a teenager and just beginning to accept that I was queer. I haven't listened to it for several years. Greg Laswell, 'What a Day'. The forgotten lyrics suddenly appear from somewhere inside me. The song speaks of all my experiences today. I get goose bumps. The day can't become any stranger. The day can't become more special. I repeat the lyrics and close my eyes. I try to relax my body although my mind resists. I feel a need to relax. I'm no longer alert. I begin to daydream. Fia is by my side. She smiles. We're alone. We know nobody around us. This never happens back home. A warm breeze hits our bodies. The sun is shining down on us. We sit on a small, grass-covered hill-top, gazing towards the sea. We see the Golden Gate Bridge. San Francisco. It truly is a day for San Francisco, just as the Laswell song says. Then the music changes.

#CrimsonandClover

01.08

My fantasy has taken me to a faraway world and I've calmed down. I get a text and remember that I'm in Greenland. A friend congratulates me on my niece and invites me out. I'm thrilled and accept immediately. I'm not yet prepared to call it a day. I already know that I won't see Fia in town. The day has given me so many surprises that it would be just too much if she appeared out of the blue. But then again, here's to hoping. I get ready and go to the club Manhattan to meet my friends. They're standing outside as I get out of the taxi. They all hug and congratulate me. I'm so proud that I can't help smiling. We walk inside and my eyes keep a lookout for the beautiful face. I can't see her but I'm not upset. I realise that something in me has changed today. Life is so wonderful that I'm not going to be sad that I can't have everything. We dance and laugh till the club closes. I smile at everybody who smiles. I hug people I haven't seen for ages. The child has filled me with so much love that I have something left to pass on. I spread love because my heart feels like it's literally overflowing. We follow my friends' friends, who have invited us to an after-party because all the nightclubs are closing. It's light and pleasant outside. We head over to a block of flats. We go in and sit down on the sofas. People talk animatedly to one another and I walk around, chatting a bit with everybody.

'Sara, come and play something on the guitar. You're so good!' my friend says.

I automatically demur. Yet the joy I have often faked feels genuine and tonight my reluctance disappears. I pick up the guitar and begin to play Greenlandic songs. The others join in singing, giving it everything they've got. Every time we start a new song, we sing it louder than the previous one. I can't help noticing a young man sitting opposite me. There's something familiar about his face and I wonder if I've met him somewhere before. He's handsome. There's something about his body language I recognise but I can't think where I would have met him. I can see that he's gay and think that I might have noticed him at Pride. Just as I'm about to ask him, he gets up and walks towards the door. I'm smiling among happy people, waiting for him to come back. It's been a long time since I've felt alive; it's a long time since I've been myself. I look around when something catches my eye. I see *her*. I see her standing next to this handsome man. She's simply so beautiful that I know I'm in love. I cannot give up, even if I have to fight for her for the rest of my life. Fia. So many things have happened all through this long day but I just can't believe that *this* is actually happening. I get up and go over to her. I'm ready to sacrifice my light heart.

She'll either accept it or reject it. Either way, it's worth it. I just smile because I can't find the words to speak. Fia is also silent. I can't figure out what she's thinking. I've sacrificed my precious heart and all I can do is hope that it won't be ruined. She hands me a crumpled piece of paper; I unfold it and read. Our song.

I sing it. I sing it just for *her*.

The spring morning comes alive. The blue sky lights up. The rays of the sun hit Sermitsiaq and the north-eastern spring sky shines red. The morning is still. The morning is gentle. The air is fresh and I stand right in front of Fia. I gaze at her. Hear her. Touch her. Kiss her. I want to spend all my time with her. I feel her. I love her.

'Crimson and Clover,' I say to her.

'Over and over,' she replies.

What a day to be alive, I think.

04.32

#whataday

Glossary

Angaju: affectionate name for an older same-sex sibling

Arnaq: woman (also a common name for women)

Arnbitter: bitter herbal liqueur like Jägermeister or Fernet-Branca

Carlsberg, Classic: brands of Danish beer

French hotdog: a hotdog in which a sausage is inserted into a hole in a special style of bread/bun

Hotel Godthåb: a bar in Nuuk named after the colonial Danish name for Nuuk

Iggu: sweet/cute, or 'sweetie'

Ilimmarfik: the University of Greenland, situated in Nuuk

Inatsisartut: the parliament of Greenland

Inuk: human/man, mankind (also a common name for men)

Inuugit: live your life

Inuuneq: life

Inuunera: my life

Ivik/Ivinnguaq: a blade of grass (also a common name for women and men)

KNR: the national Greenlandic radio and TV station

Kolonihavnen: an old harbour from the colonial period (around the seventeenth century). Now a place for Sunday walks, sightseeing, artisanal shops, the national museum and national events

Kujallerpaat: a street name

Manhattan: nightclub in Nuuk

Naamik: no

Nuussuaq: a district of Nuuk

Qinngorput: a new district of Nuuk

Sermitsiaq: mountain outside Nuuk and the city's landmark

Sermitsiaq.ag: website of a Greenlandic newspaper-house

Sticky pig's tails: an inexpensive dish typically made from cheap meat

21 June: a national holiday

About the Author

Niviaq Korneliussen was born in 1990 in Nuuk and grew up in South Greenland. She studied psychology at Aarhus University in Denmark and spent a year in California as an exchange student. Korneliussen started writing in 2013 and is the winner of many writing competitions. Her debut novel, *Crimson*, was first published under the title *HOMO sapienne* in 2014. She translated it herself from Greenlandic to Danish. She is currently working on her second novel.